13.40

Emden, Cecil Stuart.

Pepys himself

DATE DUE			

PEPYS HIMSELF

CECIL S. EMDEN

Pepys Himself

GREENWOOD PRESS, PUBLISHERS
WESTPORT. CONNECTICUT

Library of Congress Cataloging in Publication Data

Emden, Cecil Stuart.
    Pepys himself.

    Reprint of the ed. published by Oxford
University Press, London.
    Includes index.
    1. Pepys, Samuel, 1633-1703--Biography--
Character. 2. Statesmen--Great Britain--Biography.
3   Authors, English--Early modern, 1500-1700
--Biography. I. Title.
[DA447.P4E45 1980]   941.06'6'0924 [B] 80-17177
ISBN 0-313-22607-5 (lib. bdg.)

Reprinted in 1980 by Greenwood Press,
A division of Congressional Information Service, Inc.
88 Post Road West, Westport, Connecticut 06881

Printed in the United States of America

10 9 8 7 6 5 4 3 2 1

FOR H.N.E. AND A.B.E.

Contents

Introductory

The usual method of writing about Samuel Pepys is biographical, with incidental remarks about his character. The present brief sketch reverses the emphasis, dealing primarily with character, and including only a minimum of biographical particulars. This procedure is intended to provide advantageous opportunities for appreciating Pepys's personal qualities, and for viewing them in due proportion.

Information about his motives in his dealings with other people, which he reveals with unexampled candour in the Diary, is scattered among a mass of material useful to political, social, and naval historians, and to biographers. It is also to be found in his accounts of everyday occupations, gossip, and matters of transient interest. An attempt is made here to analyse and comment on much of the evidence indicating the kind of man that Pepys was, so as to facilitate acquaintance with this enigmatical, intriguing, and remarkable person.

This sketch is based almost entirely on the Diary, and is thus confined to the years 1660–69. For the post-Diary period, the available information is relatively slight; and it is more inferential, the chief source being the correspondence. Only a small proportion of his many surviving letters, most of them concerned with Admiralty business, throw any light on his disposition. A study of Pepys, the man, extending from youth to age, would prove a difficult subject for a book, since the evidence would be uneven in both quantity and quality. There is much to be said for confining attention to the period of the Diary, for, although a view of him obtained from this illustrious source alone will not be comprehensive, it will be homogeneous. The material used will be of consistent reliability. This does not mean that discrimination is not requisite. The diarist, for instance, while uniformly honest about himself, is apt to be introspective, and excessively concerned with self-examination. He sometimes seems to be paying as much attention to recording his defects as to describing incidents which might illustrate his admirable qualities.

The letters suffer from the disadvantage of including only occasional evidence of the kind required here; and they are more difficult than the Diary to interpret. It is obvious that, in some of them, Pepys, like numerous other letter-writers, was anxious to exhibit himself in favourable aspects, whereas, in the Diary, he is always frank, being free from any affectation or constraint. There, his intentness on self-expression promotes a realistic appreciation: it involves the disclosure of unattractive as well as attractive features. Nevertheless, the letters must not be neglected in pursuing the present purpose. Even if due allowance is made for some self-consciousness or disingenuousness, they contain a large number of passages from which a reasonable person must imply a decidedly pleasing image of the writer. In his prime, he undoubtedly deserved the unqualified respect shown him by several distinguished and perceptive friends.

When acting in his professional capacity, especially at the periods when he was Secretary of the Admiralty, after the conclusion of the Diary, Pepys may be said to disclose himself in his correspondence as kindly, courteous, and patient, with a sympathetic understanding of human problems. There are few imperfections discernible; and, for a highly placed Civil Servant, who had risen quickly to a position of considerable authority, his letters give but small indication of a sense of self-importance. It is true that he enjoyed wielding power and maintaining discipline; but he acted in these respects with moderation and forbearance. He was only rigorous and peremptory when an offender had an air of impertinence, or showed gross disregard for the interest of the Navy. In his private correspondence, too, though this suffered from the formality of the age, he can constantly be found to be concerned with other people's troubles, especially those of his relations.

A cursory reading of the Diary is sufficient to make it all too obvious that, at that period, he was not free from serious failings; but it may safely be assumed that he mellowed with age; and, in later life, he attained to a notable degree of both tolerance and self-mastery. His pleasant qualities became more noticeable; and he must have succeeded in curbing those that are undesirable.

Pepys was twenty-six years old when he started keeping a diary, and thirty-six when his defective eyesight forced him to give up writing it. It covers more than a third of his most active years, a period when he can be said to have been in his prime, though he was not yet at the height of his career and influence. This does not mean that a portrait based on the Diary must needs be an inadequate or misleading one, provided we remember that he had not at this stage reached the full measure of either his sensibility or his prudence.

For the present purpose, the earlier years are of special consequence, for, during them, he rose to be an important personage; and, during them, too, the main story of his married life is revealed with extraordinary outspokenness. What, indeed, can be more significant of character than progress in matrimony? Seldom, if ever, has so much been known of the inner mind of a diarist, so that we must by no means be dissatisfied if this unique source does not cover a longer period.

NOTE

The quotations from the Diary are taken from the edition by Henry B. Wheatley, first published in 1893–99. The publishers of this edition are Messrs. George Bell and Sons, Ltd.

I

Good Fortune

'His disposition was lively and social, his feelings highly sensitive, his temper quickly excitable, his passions and affections warm.' This assessment of Pepys was written in 1833, about eight years after the first publication of extracts from the Diary. Naturally, little had been said by then about the man himself in the light of his self-disclosures. But this early attempt is remarkably perspicuous; and it would be difficult to say anything more accurate in as few words.

It is proposed to illustrate, in the following pages, these and other features. The sensitiveness of his temperament, and his consequent tendency to break out into excited language, must be borne in mind; and we shall fail in comprehending his character if we do not give these features due consideration. Among other significant aspects, his lively ambition must have prominent notice. His circumstances favoured this disposition, for, though, as a youngster, his station was a humble one,[1] he soon came to realize that he had exceptional talents, and that, by good fortune, he had gained admirable opportunities in which to exercise them.

In June 1660, through the influence of his kinsman and patron, the Earl of Sandwich, he was appointed a Commissioner and a Principal Officer of the Navy Board, as Clerk of the Acts. It was not long before it became plain to him that he had been remarkably

[1] He came of good family, the Pepyses of Cottenham, in Cambridgeshire.

lucky in gaining this honourable and reasonably well-paid post. He delighted in his ability to exact obedience and deference; respect was due and was paid to him; and his colleagues, with whom he would consort, were men with distinguished service in the Navy, or in naval administration. When admitted to their friendship he would have social advantages, if not of an eminent kind, at least of a kind which, shortly before, he had not regarded as being within his reach; and social prestige was to prove almost as important to him as material prosperity.

A little investigation convinced him that his status as Principal Officer and Clerk of the Acts had, in the past, been regarded as equal to that of his colleagues, in spite of the fact that he had to perform secretarial duties. This was in accordance with old traditions; but the situation was less clear than it might have been, because the post had been in abeyance during the Commonwealth. One or two of his colleagues were inclined to suggest that, as Clerk of the Acts, his duties were primarily to prepare and record business, and to draft letters and instructions. Pepys quickly realized that he must insist on his equality with the others, and on taking a full part in the decisions of the Board. But it was not for many months that he envisaged himself as a forceful member. And it was certainly a longer period still before it seemed possible that he might become the most dynamic and enterprising member of them all, an achievement reached by the end of the period of the Diary. Moreover, it took him some time and trouble to understand that his post might prove more lucrative than at first appeared likely, and that there were customary perquisites available whereby he and his colleagues could supplement their salaries very considerably. He was to find that money was not merely useful in securing esteem. It was essential to a successful career.

For the first year or more of his professional activities Pepys was by no means single-minded in his attention to business. This was partly due to competing interests. The private affairs of Lord Sandwich, with which he was frequently entrusted, social activities, and a notable indulgence in conviviality and playgoing occupied a good deal of his time. He also held for a few months a temporary additional post as a Clerk of the Privy Seal. Moreover, a number of his mornings or afternoons, and even whole days, were spent on supervising the alterations and improvements to his official residence, a subject which he found to be of absorbing interest. At that stage, his attendances at his office and at Whitehall cannot have amounted to more than four half-days a week. But it is fair to remark that some of the time spent in social activity must have proved to be remunerative, as he gained thereby some valuable business contacts.

It was not until the end of 1661 that he decided that his welfare and happiness demanded that he should devote himself whole-heartedly to the interests of the Navy. By this time he not only saw the folly of frittering away his days, but he had also begun to recognize the extent to which he might strengthen his personal position on the Navy Board. In the following years he was sedulous in his duties, and enterprising in his interpretation of them. After this sudden transformation, there were but few and brief periods in which pleasure or his own personal pursuits beguiled him unduly. But, as he frequently admitted in the Diary, the claims of pleasure were now and then overwhelmingly alluring and insistent. He seems to have felt that he was at all times apt to be peculiarly at the mercy of the enticements of women, wine, and dissipation in general. It may well be that there was much truth in this; and it is also likely that it was only by keeping the benefits of assiduity prominently in his mind that he succeeded in making ample use of his talents and opportunities.

Although it took some time for Pepys to realize the extent of the openings available to him for becoming an influential public servant, and incidentally for accumulating a useful private fortune, he was quick to enjoy the dignity and respect that his appointment warranted. Recognition of his importance by subordinates which was momentarily embarrassing to him soon became a matter of gratification when he visited naval dockyards. During an early visit to Deptford, he began to feel 'the great authority of my place, and was treated with so much respect and honour that I was at a loss how to behave myself'. A little later, at Chatham, 'I find that I begin to know how to receive so much reverence, which at the beginning I could not tell how to do'. Then, at Woolwich, he proceeded a stage further: 'I perceive people do begin to value me, and that I shall be able to command in all matters.' In the circumstances of his sudden advance in status, this naïve sense of satisfaction was excusable.

It took him longer, being a novice, to be able to discuss technicalities with the experienced members of the Navy Board, all much his senior in age. Gradually, however, he showed them that he was gaining a considerable grasp of the supply service of the Navy. He was extremely quick at picking up new information. 'I . . . do not see but every body begins to give me as much respect and honour as any of the rest.' And he was delighted to notice that, as he walked 'by brave moonshine' from a dockyard towards London, three or four armed men were appointed to guard him.

In his office, too, he was establishing a reputation, and was becoming known not only as easily accessible, but helpful. 'I am very well entered into the business and esteem of the office, and do ply it close, and find benefit by it.' People began to ask for him by name. In this way he acquired much useful technical knowledge in discussions with such visitors as contractors, commanders of ships, and minor officials. Two days running he recorded that he was up early at his office, 'where people come to me about business', and 'I find all people beginning to come to me'.

Not long after he began to understand how he could, with advantage to the Navy and to himself, apply his entire energies whole-heartedly to his profession, he gained the favour and approval of two influential members of the Navy Board, Sir George Carteret and William (later Sir William) Coventry. Both were powerful at Court. The former had long administrative experience, and a strong claim on the King's goodwill. The latter was a man of quick mind and considerable intellectual ability. His genuine devotion to the public interest was exceptional; and, as Secretary to the Duke of York, the Lord High Admiral, he was in a favourable position to advance the interests of a hard-working and enterprising member of the Board.

Carteret was soon speaking well of Pepys to the Lord Chancellor and others; and Coventry told Lord Sandwich that Pepys was 'indeed the life of the office'. Lord Sandwich assisted the growth of his prestige by securing his appointment as a member of the Tangier Commission. With support such as this he felt assured that he was launched on a most promising career; and he concluded that 'on all hands, by God's blessing, I find myself a very rising man'. By the end of 1662 he could write: 'By my last year's diligence in my office, blessed be God! I am come to a good degree of my knowledge therein; and am acknowledged so by all the world, even the Duke [of York] himself to whom I have good access: . . . and I doubt not but, by the continuance of the same endeavours, I shall in a little time come to be a man much taken notice of in the world, specially being come to so great an esteem with Mr. Coventry.'

Pepys's growing success in his profession can be largely attributed to three factors. He proved himself assiduous and painstaking. He was enterprising in gaining a wide and practical understanding of the supply service of the Navy, and its need for reformation. And his cleverness in personal relations, especially in ingratiating himself with the most influential people, was an essential feature in his advancement. He could, therefore, record with truth and well-grounded satisfaction: 'I have good content in mind to see myself improve every day in knowledge and being known.' His continued progress must be attributed, not only to the above-mentioned qualities, but also to his outstanding ability as an administrator, which developed steadily with experience.

2

Tensions

———————————————————————

Sir William Penn and Sir William Batten, two colleagues of Pepys whose official residences were in the same range of buildings as his own, in Seething Lane, and with whom he spent a good many convivial evenings during the first months of his appointment, occupy prominent places in the Diary. They were both admirals, well practised in their profession. Penn was much the younger, and had learnt some of his professional skill from Batten. Of the two, Penn was clearly the more competent, at any rate at the stage of the Diary.

Pepys soon found reason to be suspicious of them, and constantly pictures them as crooked. In his view, not only did they treat him disingenuously, but they benefited their pockets at the expense of the Service by conniving at malpractices, by making dubious profits, and by accepting presents from contractors to an improper extent, or in improper circumstances. Within certain ill-defined limits, money or other gifts could be justifiably accepted from contractors by public servants in recognition of their patronage and influence. But it was generally understood that it was illicit to receive money in consideration of unnecessarily high prices being paid for goods, or in consideration of the acceptance of goods of deficient quality. Pepys was accustomed to disparage and even vilify the two admirals if they opposed his interests, or interfered with his claims to privileges or to equality of status with them. In these circumstances, he would characterize them in opprobrious terms. As time went on he himself frequently accepted presents from contractors, but he steadily alleged that his behaviour was in no way contrary to the King's interest, and that often, by his astuteness, he ensured good quality in goods and reasonableness in price.

Some pleasure may be gained in speculating how far Pepys was correct in his description of Penn and Batten as dishonest in the sense of transgressing the accepted standards, as well as perfidious, and how far his feelings carried him away and made him exaggerate. An even more interesting subject is the extent to which Pepys himself overstepped the proper limits of professional good conduct.

Besides being in general the more able of the two, Penn was much the more quick-witted, and was, at the period of the Diary, at the height of his powers. He was certainly shrewd, probably crafty, and possibly double-faced. During the Civil War he seems to have tried to 'play safe', serving the Parliamentarians for long periods at sea, and at the same time being ready to ingratiate himself with King Charles II over the water. Pepys, who in his more impartial moments acknowledged that Penn was highly efficient, could also describe him as 'very cunning'. There were several people with naval experience, among them Lord Sandwich, who considered that Penn had sometimes proved himself to be unreliable. On the other hand, Coventry, a man of integrity, befriended him.

At the time of the Diary, Batten was past his prime. He could hardly be described as sly, for his was a simple character. His record in the Civil War was much less questionable than that of Penn. He was no turncoat, being, as far as practicable, a steady Royalist.[1] His service under the Parliamentarians was brief, and not such as to compromise his loyalty to the King. During Cromwell's régime he held no naval appointment. On settling down to the life of a Commissioner of the Navy Board after the Restoration, he lived in sumptuous fashion. He evidently meant to make as large

[1] The suggestion that he acted in opposition to Charles I does not seem to be borne out by the evidence.

profits in his office as he could with safety; and he was angry if anyone tried to thwart him.

There is a portrait of Penn by Lely which suggests that he had a sensitive, kindly face, with a sincere expression; and we must be prepared to think that his duplicity may well have been exaggerated by people who had cause to dislike him. Batten, it is clear, was easily given to sudden bursts of anger. We may guess that his face was rubicund, being coloured by the weather, by alcoholic liquor, and occasionally also by strong feelings. An effective impression of his portly figure has been left us by King Charles II, as quoted by Pepys. The King 'swore merrily that he believed that the ketch that Sir W. Batten bought the last year at Colchester was of his own getting [begetting], it was so thick to its length'.

Both the admirals were, as is obvious from the Diary, amiable and even benevolent, as well as being uncommonly sociable. Relations between them and Pepys were sometimes cordial, sometimes only apparently cordial, and sometimes unambiguously strained and even unfriendly.

During the first few months in office social activity between the three of them was experimental, and did not extend to their families. There were frequent meetings at the nearby tavern, where they drank freely, told lively stories, and indulged in jollification. In these circumstances, Pepys found Penn to be 'a merry fellow and pretty good natured, and sings very bawdy songs', and to be 'very good company'.

The two admirals were hard and experienced drinkers; and Pepys's first instinct was to be on terms of good fellowship. They seemed strongly inclined to a similar course, not wishing Pepys to take his duties too seriously. They hoped to find him manageable and compliant. And the continuation of the relationship of boon-companions at the tavern would have suited them excellently.

Unfortunately, where alcohol was concerned, Pepys was weak in two respects. He found it easy to drink more than was wise; and wine seemed to have a deleterious effect on his constitution. A drinking bout, besides upsetting his stomach, left his head 'troubled'; it ached all night after a debauch, and sometimes the next day so much so that he could describe himself as unfit for business. Temptations to indulge in carousals were considerable, emanating from other sources besides his fellow Commissioners. There were associates of his who liked to persuade him to drink all the afternoon, or till late at night, consuming large quantities of sack or Rhenish wine.

After a few months this phase of excessive drinking seems to have produced in him some uneasiness of conscience; and he described it as 'my great folly'. But for some time he found no adequate incentive to put a limit to this addiction, and he merely remarked: 'Finding my head grow weak now-a-days if I come to drink wine, and therefore hope that I shall leave it off myself which I pray God I could do.' He was particularly troubled at the thriftlessness which his behaviour involved; but, even though he had a very keen sense of the value of money, this alone was insufficient to restrain him.

Towards the end of 1661 he came to recognize with full force that he could not allow his professional prospects and personal happiness to be endangered any longer by dissipation. He was learning to appreciate the extent to which his prestige, and possibly his income, could be enlarged by a display of efficiency and enterprise. As a result, he entered upon a system of solemn vows, the breach of which would involve him in the payment of monetary forfeits, so much to be put into the poor-box in respect of such and such transgressions. Soon he could write that 'since my leaving drinking of wine, I do find myself much better and do mind my business better and do spend less money, and less time lost in idle company'. The change was dramatic; and it was, in the main, effective and lasting. He applied the same system to playgoing, which he also found to be a too captivating diversion. As a result, he could claim to have extricated himself from these allurements. 'My mind is now in a wonderful condition of quiet and content, more than ever in my life since my minding the business of my office, which I have done most constantly; and I find it to be the very effect of my late oaths against wine and plays, which, if God please, I will keep constant in, for now my business is a delight to me, and brings me great credit, and my purse encreases too.'

The foregatherings of Pepys, Penn, and Batten at the tavern achieved their thorough mutual acquaintance. When these social occasions had served this purpose, first the Battens and then the Penns offered Pepys and his wife warm welcomes to their homes. At the Battens, they 'were much made of'. So friendly did the two families become that Batten chose Mrs. Pepys for his Valentine, and gave her half a dozen pairs of gloves and a pair of silk stockings and garters for her Valentine's gift. Pepys responded with gifts for Batten's daughter, but with less enthusiasm. In the spring of 1661 the Pepyses were dining with the Battens about once a week; and were also invited to their country home.

Pepys found that this extreme familiarity had an unsatisfactory effect on his professional position. Batten, he thought, wished to use hospitality as a means by which he could patronize him, and treat him almost as a young relation. In this way he could make it difficult for Pepys to oppose him in office matters. As a result of Pepys's appreciation of this situation, he managed to ensure that the pace of social activity slackened notably. He decided to 'make myself a great stranger, only to get a high opinion a little more of myself in them'. On another occasion, he said: 'I am resolved to keep myself more reserved, to avoyd the contempt which otherwise I must fall into . . .'

Meanwhile the meetings between Pepys and Penn had been chiefly in male company, or *à deux*. Nevertheless an intimacy was developing in their friendship. An incident which took place in the summer of 1661 illustrates the easy and comfortable terms that then existed. 'After dinner to the office, where we sat and did business, and Sir W. Pen and I went home with Sir R. Slingsby to bowls in his ally, and there had good sport, and afterwards went in and drank and talked. So home Sir William and I, and it being very hot weather I took my flageolette and I played upon the leads in the garden, where Sir W. Pen came out in his shirt into his leads, and there we staid talking and singing, and drinking great drafts of claret, and eating botargo and bread and butter till 12 at night, it being moonshine; and so to bed, very near fuddled.'

The dangers inherent in a great deal of social activity between families like the Penns and the Pepyses, with husbands likely to be involved in rivalries and contention in business matters, became obvious at the Christmas season of 1661. As Pepys remarked, 'much correspondence there has been between our two families all this Christmas'. Some ten times in close succession there were parties at one house or the other; occasionally dinner, in the middle of the day; more often supper in the evening, with cards as the usual entertainment, being suitable for the amusement of the Penn children. The situation proved to be entirely similar to that experienced by Pepys with the Battens. He found that his freedom of action in the office could be hampered by a high degree of intimacy with the Penns in the domestic sphere. If family meetings were only quite rare, it would be easier for Pepys to combat any challenge to his status and privileges; and he would be more free to criticize Penn's arguments or proposals on the Board, or to question any irregularities in his arrangement of contracts.

He had a warning that embarrassing circumstances of this kind might arise when he found the two Sir Williams at the office choosing Masters for a new fleet of ships. This should have been done at a 'full table', as Sir George Carteret soon pointed out. Pepys mentioned a Master whom he wished to be appointed; but Penn, who seemed to be 'in an ugly humour', refused. Naturally enough, Pepys felt that he had been slighted; and that his right to equal consultation was being threatened. Doubtless he was also indignant because patronage of this kind was often profitable in bringing presents from grateful appointees; and he was being excluded from his opportunity.

A good deal of the friction which arose from time to time between Pepys and the two Sir Williams was attributable to the attitude of the latter towards Pepys's status on the Navy Board. Penn, especially, adhered for some time to the opinion that Pepys was not entirely the equal of the others. Pepys naturally objected to being treated as subject to the supervision of the Board, or to being referred to as 'our Register'. He took this 'in some dudgeon', as he contended that he was as complete a member of the Board as they were. He saw the dangers of allowing any infringement of his rights, and remarked 'that I must keep myself at a little distance with them and not crouch or else I shall never keep myself up even with them'. He accordingly meant 'to be exact in my duty there [at the office] and exacting my privileges, and shall continue to do so'.

Matters came to a serious head in the summer of 1662, when Pepys's privilege of having the Board's contracts prepared by his clerks was challenged by Penn, who told Pepys that the Comptroller should properly have this function. Orders and precedents were looked into, and the Board ruled that Pepys's assertion was justified. Pepys felt affronted at this challenge, and suspected Penn of plotting to undermine his position. He ended his account of the incident by remarking that Penn 'did it like a base raskall, and so I shall remember him while I live'. These words sound vindictive; but Pepys was given to expressing himself in extravagant terms when he was provoked, so that they should not be taken literally. He had, however, ample grounds for being aggrieved. He treated Penn coolly for a time; and the incident rankled with him.

Not long after this conflict Pepys and his wife saw Penn and his daughter in the adjoining garden, walking near them in full view; but as 'I have lately had cause to be much prejudiced, we took no notice of them a great while'. A week or two later Penn invited the Pepyses to dinner on a Sunday, and afterwards to supper. Pepys remarked that Penn 'do much fawn upon me, and I perceive would not fall out with me . . ., but I shall never be deceived again by him, but do hate him and his traitorous tricks with all my heart'. A few days afterwards Penn came to take leave of Pepys, prior to a visit to Ireland, and offered all his services. 'I did, God forgive me! promise him all my service and love, though the rogue knows he deserves none from me, nor do I intend to show him any, but as he dissembles with me, so must I with him.'

Now and again Pepys determined to treat Penn with a minimum of familiarity. But they were often to be found behaving in a thoroughly friendly manner. It was not unusual for them to attend a play in company. Either Pepys's tactics passed unnoticed by

Penn, or he was, in fact, less cool than he made himself out to be.

For several weeks during 1662 and 1663 Penn suffered from severe attacks of gout, and was unable to move. When Pepys paid him sympathetic visits, as he often did, the conversation sometimes turned to the office; and, on two occasions, he took the opportunity of conveying to Penn his firm intention of being regarded as the equal of his colleagues, and of taking an active part in the deliberations of the Board. After some talk, he made himself 'appear one of greater action and resolution as to publique business than I have hitherto done, at which he listens, but I know he is a rogue in his heart and likes not, but I perceive I may hold up my head, and the more the better, I minding my business as I have done, in which God do and will bless me'. Later on, when Penn was about to return to his duties, Pepys gave him an account of how matters stood in the office, 'that when he comes abroad again, he may know what to think of me, and to value me as he ought'. The future administrative head of the Navy was consolidating his position. He was not only standing up for his rights, but he was proving that he had a poise and a personality that must be respected.

3

Antagonisms

Involvement in business with his colleagues confirmed Pepys in the view that social prestige was an important element in advancement. He was determined to prove that, in the social sphere, he was as well equipped as his neighbours living in the block of official residences adjacent to the office of the Navy Board. His rooms and furnishings, his hospitality, and his servants had all to be at least as creditable as theirs. When it became usual for officials of his rank to have boys in livery to attend on them as they went about their occasions, he put his boy into a fine outfit, 'very handsome', 'black and gold lace upon grey, being the colour of my arms'. The boy was soon equipped with a little sword 'to outdo Sir W. Pen's boy, who this day, and Sir W. Batten's too, begin to wear new livery; but I do take mine to be the neatest of them all'.

As Pepys raised his status on the Navy Board and succeeded in maintaining the traditional rights and privileges of his place, he became ready to proceed a step further and to criticize and attack the proposals of his colleagues if he disapproved of them. When he opposed Penn in regard to the question of fining a purser who was absent from duty without excuse, Penn was 'mighty angry'. 'At which I am never a whit sorry; I would not have him think that I dare not oppose him when I see reason and cause for it.' He even 'talked boldly' to Sir J. Minnes, the Comptroller, about a letter written by him, and was glad to do so before other members of the Board 'that they might see that I am somebody . . .'

With the passage of years, Pepys showed increasing firmness in resisting those proposals made by Penn that he considered to be unjustifiable. Penn was particularly incensed when Pepys withstood his scheme to have 'a piece of the great office cut out to make an office for him'; and a day or two afterwards 'did look mightily reservedly upon me, and still he shall do so for me, for I will be hanged before I seek to him, unless I need it'. The breach was slow to heal; and he wrote a little later regarding meetings of the Board: 'Sir W. Pen and I look much askewe one upon another, though afterward business made us speak friendly enough, but yet we hate one another.' 'Sir W. Pen looks upon me, and I on him, and speak about business together at the table well enough, but no friendship or intimacy since our late difference about his closet, nor do I desire to have any.' We may guess that Pepys was inclined to exaggerate Penn's protracted resentment, for Penn was basically of a conciliatory disposition.

Batten, like Penn, evidently disliked friction, and seems to have been even more desirous of maintaining peaceful relations. But Pepys was apt to construe Batten's attempts to renew friendly intimacy as an effort to propitiate him. Batten, he supposed, was anxious lest he should be planning to interfere with some profitable operation of his. It seems equally likely, however, that Batten, being a thoroughly good-natured man, was determined to do all he could to smooth over asperities.

After a period when the situation between them was strained, Batten invited Pepys and his wife to dinner. This Pepys regarded as 'a mighty condescension in them', and suspected some sinister design, 'or else it pleases God by my late care of business to make me more considerable even with them than I am sure they would willingly owne me to be. God make me thankfull and carefull to preserve myself so, for I am sure they hate me, and it is hope or fear that makes them flatter me.' The efforts of the Battens to ingratiate themselves were recurrent. Pepys described them as 'being nowadays very fond of me', and himself as being 'mighty great with them'.

His frequent assumption that he was hated is an interesting feature of his character; and he often exemplifies it. It may, perhaps, illustrate his self-satisfaction in his growing importance, or it may reflect a rancorous tendency in himself. Near the end of the Diary, when he described a merry dinner-party at his house, he spoke of Penn, who was a guest, as 'being on all occasions glad to be at friendship with me though we hate one another and know it on both sides'. When the Penns had been paying him delicate attentions, he was full of suspicion, for he felt that they were 'as false as the devil himself'. Nevertheless, he regarded himself as 'a happy man, that all my fellow-officers are desirous of my friendship'. It was, indeed, a considerable tribute to Pepys's ability and social qualities that Penn and Batten should be constantly anxious to renew a basis of goodwill, and to forget the dissensions that had arisen between them, for there is no doubt that Pepys's extreme sensitiveness made him a difficult colleague.

At the same time, it is possible that the placable behaviour of the two admirals towards Pepys may have been partly due to a desire to restrain him from investigating aspects of office business that would be inconvenient to them. Pepys, a few months after he had begun to be assiduous in his duties, suspected Batten's honesty in several respects. If goods supplied for the Navy were not of proper quality, it was the duty of the dockyard officials to report the facts. Pepys considered that this duty was apt to be neglected because Batten's interests were to some extent identified with those of the contractors. 'I would not', said Pepys, 'have the King's workmen discouraged (as Sir W. Batten do most basely do) from representing the faults of merchant's goods where there is any.' He also objected to Batten's supposed hole-in-the-corner way of concluding contracts, suspecting that, when the contracts were made clandestinely, they might include private terms which were not in the public interest. Batten accused Pepys of a hostile attitude towards him, and said that 'he heard that I was offended with merchants coming to his house and making contracts there. I did tell him that as a friend I had spoke of it to Sir W. Pen and desired him to take a time to tell him [Batten] of it, and not as a backbiter, with which he was satisfied, but I find that Sir W. Pen has played the knave with me, and not told it as a friend, but in a bad sense.'

There were also specific contracts which aroused Pepys's suspicions. He thought that both Penn and Batten were involved in 'some corruption' in regard to a contract for the supply of tar, 'which I am resolved to cross, though he [Batten] sent me last night, as a bribe, a barrel of sturgeon, which, it may be, I shall send back, for I will not have the King abused so abominably in the price of what we buy, by Sir W. Batten's corruption and underhand dealing'. Then there was much questioning about the quality of hemp supplied for rope-making, a subject on which Pepys devoted a great deal of energy. In a half-yearly summary of his progress in his profession, he remarked that Penn and Batten, as well as Minnes, the Comptroller, 'do rather envy me than love me, I standing in most of their lights, specially Sir W. Batten, whose cheats I do daily oppose to his great trouble, though he appears mighty kind and willing to keep friendship with me'.

Much of Pepys's invective against Penn and Batten was probably no more than a means of letting off steam, for he was, as we have noticed, of an excitable and even highly strung temperament. He can hardly have remained on what appeared to the world to be friendly and intimate terms with them for a number of years and have really intended what he wrote about them. When, for instance, he remarked 'so false a fellow as Sir W. Pen I never did nor hope shall ever know again', he may well have meant 'unreasonable' or 'unaccommodating' rather than 'false'. It is obvious that he could not bear to be crossed in business; and when his colleagues opposed him he was momentarily indignant.

Once or twice, in his descriptions of his encounters with the two admirals, he disclosed the considerable extent to which his feelings could be aroused. On arriving at the office one day, ready for a meeting of the Board, he suddenly had 'a most furious conflict' with Penn on a matter 'of no great moment, but very bitter, and stared on one another, and so broke off, and to our business, my heart as full of spite as it could hold . . .' Penn, like other sufferers from the gout, could be short of temper; and Pepys, in this and similar instances, may have displayed the same kind of lack of control that we sometimes find in his behaviour at home. The admirable realism with which he pictures the two of them staring at each other, mute with anger, is characteristic of his appreciation of significant detail.

His aggravation, sometimes short-lived, was by no means confined to Penn and Batten. Two of his colleagues who showed him great kindness, and with whom he was intimate, Sir G. Carteret and Lord Brouncker, expressed the opinion that Pepys held too many offices. As a result Carteret was designated a 'false friend', and Brouncker, who also became opposed to him in other ways, was described as 'a rotten hearted, false man as any one else I know, even as Sir W. Pen himself, and, therefore, I must beware of him accordingly . . .' In spite of Pepys's suspicions, he and Brouncker remained 'in appearance as good friends as ever, though I know he has a hatred to me in his heart'. He cannot have meant what he said about Carteret for there was no discernible interruption in their cordial relations.

Antagonism between Pepys and Batten intensified as it became increasingly apparent that Pepys intended not merely to criticize the contracts organized by Batten, but to compete for the organization of them himself. It was only natural for him, when he saw what easy profits Batten could make, to try and arrange similar transactions for his own benefit. This new phase first became apparent in regard to the supply of timber and masts for the use of the Navy. Batten had arranged some contracts with two contractors named Wood and Winter. But there was a considerable contractor in the same line of business, William (later Sir William) Warren, who was anxious to supplant Wood and Winter. He calculated that if he could ingratiate himself with the enterprising and ambitious young Pepys he could gain his ends. He showed Pepys the stocks of timber in his timber-yards, explained technicalities, philosophized with him, entertained him and gave him a noble present of a state dish and cup in silver. In an insinuating way, he spoke about Batten's 'corruption' and Wood's 'knavery'. It followed that Pepys, having made adverse and informed comments at the Navy Board about the terms of the contracts with Wood and with Winter, and the quality of their goods, was able in due course, but not without strenuous argument, to arrange for two large contracts with Warren, one for timber and the other for masts, running into thousands of pounds. As a result, Warren treated Pepys generously, with presents and payments of money.

Batten, however, did not like being outwitted; and he did not mean to lose his profits on timber contracts without a struggle. He made a stiff resistance at the Navy Board against Pepys's proposals; and much annoyed Pepys because he 'in my absence inveighed against my contract the other day for Warren's masts, in which he is a knave, and I shall find matter of tryumph, but it vexes me a little'.

It would have been more in the interests of the Navy, and would have saved some resentment, if Penn, Batten and Pepys had been able to agree who was the most desirable contractor in the public interest, and had been satisfied with equal shares in any present that the chosen contractor thought prudent to give in recognition of past kindnesses and in expectation of future ones. But this sensible compromise would have been unworkable if for no other reason than that it would imply a considerable degree of mutual confidence.

However, after a few years of occasional rivalry and consequent discord, all three of them came to recognize that there were certain phases of profiteering in which partnership was feasible and desirable. Their talents could be pooled, and also the pickings. They accordingly joined together in plans for making some money from naval prizes. After dinner with Batten one day, Pepys discussed with him 'how to get ourselves into the prize office [as Commissioners of Prize] or some other fair way of obliging the King to consider us in our extraordinary pains'. Later, he had some friendly discourse with Batten ('though I will never trust him far') about the prospects of the three of them getting the loan of a privateer, *The Flying Greyhound*. He did not think that the King would deny them. The King did not, though it is difficult to see how he justified this curious and probably illicit financial venture on the part of these three Navy Commissioners. When there was a prospect of securing a more permanent interest in *The Flying Greyhound* it seems that Penn proved himself to be untrustworthy. Batten told Pepys that Penn had got an order in respect of the ship for himself only, 'which is so false a thing, and the part of a knave, as nothing almost can be more'. On Pepys asking Penn for an explanation of this apparent breach of faith, he was 'much disturbed, and would excuse it at the most he can, but do so so basely, that though he do offer to let go his pretence to her, and resign up his order for her, and come in only to ask his share of her, . . . yet I shall remember him for a knave while I live'. This incident exemplifies the difficulties inherent in maintaining harmony among partners engaged in dubious enterprises, especially where the partners were temperamentally unsuited to such collaboration.

About the same time, and shortly after the Great Fire of London, Penn, during a moonlight walk in the garden, proposed to Pepys that they might make some money together by buying up Scottish timber and selling it at a profit to those who had to rebuild their burnt houses. At first the prospects seemed to them to be good; but this not very reputable scheme, which involved taking advantage of the plight of some unfortunate people, did not mature, because the prospective partners were advised against it, as being unlikely to be financially successful.

The frequent close personal relations of contractors with some of the members of the Navy Board tended to encourage in these officials an interest in commercial enterprises. There was presumably no law against such transactions by officials. But they must have been apt to divert attention from naval business. The inclination to be constantly looking for ways of making money was widely prevalent among those holding senior public appointments. It can, we may suppose, be largely explained by the precariousness of office.

4

Expediency

The tactics which Pepys adopted in regard to his association with his colleagues changed with added experience of problems and personalities. At first, he took the obvious course, and tried to be on good terms with everybody. 'I perceive', he observed caustically, 'that none of our officers care much for one another, but I keep in with them all as much as I can.' By 1662, Sir George Carteret and William Coventry, both aristocrats and powerful in Court circles (in contrast with Minnes, Penn, and Batten, who were middle-class ex-naval commanders), were making their influence felt on the Board. Pepys rightly supposed that if he could gain the favour of these two important persons they would be able to support him in his endeavours to improve the efficiency of naval administration; and thus his prestige would be enhanced. As a result, he would have his hand strengthened in dealing with those of his colleagues who were apt to thwart him.

Pepys decided 'to keep much in with Sir George'; and he soon concluded: 'Upon the whole, I do find that he do much esteem me, and is my friend, and I may make good use of him.' The defects of Batten came up in discussion between them, and Carteret seems to have assented to the suggestion of Batten's decreasing competence. But Coventry, who was not a person to harm a well-intentioned old naval officer of sound Royalist allegiance unless compelled to do so, was less willing to agree with Pepys on this subject. He told Pepys that Batten was obviously struggling to look after his business, and, later, that 'it might be only his heaviness and unaptness for business, that he do things without advice and rashly, and to gratify people that do eat and drink and play with him . . .' Pepys evidently felt that he might have given the impression that he had some grudge against Batten; and he asked Coventry whether he thought he was acting 'out of ill will or design'. Coventry, however, reassured him. Meanwhile, poor Batten suspected that some plot was being hatched against him, and told Pepys that he had noticed that he was 'sorting himself with others'. 'Upon the whole,' wrote Pepys, somewhat heartlessly, 'I do see he perceives himself tottering, and that he is suspected, and would be kind to me, but I do my business in the office and neglect him.'

The fact was that Pepys was determined to do all he could to secure the supersession of Batten, largely, no doubt, because he was persuaded that this course would be for the benefit of the Navy. How far Batten was incompetent it is not easy to judge, but there are records which indicate that his activity was considerable. It is obvious that Pepys believed that Batten's transactions with contractors were often to the detriment of the King's service. He discussed with Penn Batten's 'suspicious dealings, wherein I was open, and he sufficiently, so that I do not care for his telling of tales, for he said as much, but whether that were so or no, I said nothing but what is my certain knowledge and belief concerning him'.

Coventry, as the Duke of York's secretary, as well as a member of the Navy Board, was a most desirable person for Pepys to cultivate; and he worked hard and successfully to this end. Coventry showed generous appreciation of Pepys's enterprise, skill, and zealous attention to his duties, and gave him every encouragement. He recommended Pepys warmly to the Duke. Soon after the time when Pepys started working strenuously at his office, Lord Sandwich told him how much he was beholden to the Duke of York, 'who did yesterday of his own accord tell him [Sandwich] that he did thank him for one person brought into the Navy, naming myself, and much more to my commendation, which is the greatest comfort and encouragement that ever I had in my life, and do owe it all to Mr. Coventry's goodness and ingenuity'.

Lord Sandwich, too, whose influence in the early stages of Pepys's career was essential to his success, treated him with increasing consideration, since he saw that he was 'respected in the world'. Some time after the encouraging remarks just quoted his patron told him that the Duke had 'the greatest love and respect and value of me that can be thought which overjoys me', and also remarked that the Duke gave 'a character of me to be a man whose industry and discretion he would trust as soon as any man's in England'.

At the battle of Lowestoft in 1665, and again in the following year, Sir William Penn acted with outstanding efficiency. As a result, he advanced markedly in the Duke's favour. It behoved Pepys, therefore, to make a quick change in tactics; and, for a spell, he found it politic to treat Penn with deference and a pretence of cordiality. Penn, on a return from service in the Fleet, dined with Pepys. 'And though I do not love him, yet I find it necessary to keep in with him; his good service . . . being much taken notice of, and reported to the King and Duke. . . . Therefore I think it discretion, great and necessary discretion, to keep in with him.'

One evening a few days later Pepys walked in the garden with Penn, 'with whom I am of late mighty great, and it is wisdom to continue myself so, for he is of all men of the office at present most manifestly useful and best thought of'. During these conversations Penn gave Pepys an account of the late naval actions and his comments on them. Pepys, in rather patronizing terms, remarked: 'He did talk very rationally to me, insomuch that I took more pleasure this night in hearing him discourse, than I ever did in my life in any thing he said.' This does not necessarily reflect adversely on Penn's ability in regard to naval administration. After all, his reputation was chiefly that of a naval commander in action.

An extraordinary aspect of the relations between Pepys and the two admirals is the apparent coexistence of a considerable amount of discord and a seemingly cheerful exchange of hospitality and courtesies. There were frequent spontaneous kindnesses shown by both sides, especially perhaps on Penn's and Batten's, in times of illness and difficulty. Not long after Pepys had moved into his official quarters, but long enough to have had some brushes with these two colleagues, he did not hesitate to borrow a cauldron of coal from one and £40 from the other. When Batten was ill, Pepys frequently called to see him; and he was constant in his attentions to Penn when he was laid up with severe attacks of gout, sometimes stopping to play cards with him. Similarly, when Pepys was ill both Penn and Batten displayed keen anxiety to give practical help. On one occasion Batten supplied juniper water, and on another 'Epsum' water, both of which seemed to do the patient good. There was also an incident where Pepys, being ill, fancied that the movement of riding in a coach tended to improve his condition. On hearing this, Penn immediately gave orders for his own coach to be got ready (Pepys not having one at that time), and drove with him almost as far as Bow.

In two instances the Battens came to Pepys's aid in awkward predicaments. When he was in danger of arrest, in circumstances where he was only nominally responsible, the Battens showed much solicitude for his welfare, and induced him to take sanctuary secretly in their house. And at the time of the Great Fire, when everyone in Pepys's situation was anxious to find means of transporting their valuables and best furniture into the country, Lady Batten sent Pepys a cart at four o'clock in the morning.

It is noticeable that, at times when relations were, according to Pepys, particularly strained, he was prepared to accept small favours, such as a lift in a coach or even a seat at a play. Penn and Batten were constantly offering small kindnesses; and although it is fair to say that he could not decently refuse them, it seems a pity that these incidents did not much serve to modify his bitter feelings towards his complaisant colleagues.

Penn, on one or two occasions, used his influence in Pepys's favour in matters of some importance to him; and Pepys did not seem to have felt any embarrassment at the acceptance of these benefits. Early in 1667 he had been crossing swords with Penn at Board meetings; but a few weeks later he asked Penn to speak with

Sir William Coventry so as to help to secure an appointment for his brother-in-law. Penn did what was necessary, and Pepys admitted, in the Diary, that the successful achievement of his object was due to Penn's intervention. But, in a later entry, he wrote grudgingly of 'the false rogue' for whom this exercise of patronage was 'a thing easy to do'. Later in the same year Penn offered to support Pepys's petition to the King, through the Duke of York, for a grant to him of a small ship in view of his good services. The petition succeeded. It can, doubtless, be alleged that Penn had selfish reasons for acting in this way. He may have been particularly anxious at that time to maintain cordial relations with Pepys. But the fact remains that he went to the trouble of helping a colleague who had sometimes been a source of annoyance to him.

There is little doubt that the relations between Pepys and the two Sir Williams were governed more by expediency than by good nature. Tactics could become highly complicated because the interests of the parties depended partly on being well thought of by the Duke of York, the Lord High Admiral, partly on the struggle to obtain a large share of the presents and profits available from contractors, and partly, as far as Pepys was concerned, on his desire to maintain the prestige of his post and to increase his personal reputation. It was not long before Pepys found that he could out-manoeuvre the simple-minded Batten; but Penn was a tougher proposition. He combined talent, technical ability, and agility of mind; and he had influence with Coventry and the Duke. Stealing a march on him was by no means easy.

5

Loyalties

The friendship between Pepys and the two admirals, if it can be so described, was, as we have seen, superficial. If they were ill, or in some minor domestic trouble, Pepys would give them his sympathy, or even his assistance. But he would hardly have regarded himself as being under an obligation to help them in any professional embarrassments. Once or twice he actually took a delight in their dilemmas. He had, in fact, no feeling of loyalty towards them. On the other hand, there were two or three distinguished people to whom he owed debts of gratitude for launching him and supporting him in the early days of his career. He appreciated that he must be loyal to these. How loyal was he? The standard at which he aimed was high; but he did not always succeed in reaching it.

Lord Sandwich was, of course, the most notable if not the most eminent of his benefactors. He not only used his influence freely in Pepys's favour, but, being a cousin by marriage, he treated him with affection and respect. And this treatment gave him just the confidence he needed in his début in public life. Unfortunately for Pepys, Sandwich was extravagant in his expenditure, and was frequently in financial straits. He was thus compelled from time to time to ask Pepys for a loan or some other financial accommodation. This was a good deal to expect of a young man who was trying to lay the foundations of an estate which might form an insurance against insecurity of employment. On the other hand, it is unlikely that, without his patron's aid, Pepys would have had an opportunity to utilize his considerable talents. Indeed, it may fairly be asserted that he owed everything to the start in life gained as a result of his appointments to the Navy Board and to the Tangier Commission; and these were entirely the result of his patron's activity.

As early as 1661 Pepys became bound as a security in a loan of £1,000 to Sandwich. At that time the risk of having to foot this bill seemed negligible; and, in any case, Pepys was not at that time worth anything like that sum. Soon, too, he began to lend money to Lord Sandwich; and by 1663 these loans amounted to £700, in fact to most of his savings at that time. From that period onwards Sandwich's financial position steadily deteriorated; and his reputation may have suffered a little in some circles as a result of its being generally known that he was spending much of his time with a lady in Chelsea, and, as a consequence, was failing to attend at Court with proper regularity. Pepys probably gained a distorted impression of the seriousness of this affair. After much hesitation, he wrote to his patron a letter of protest couched in humble and delicate phraseology, in which he made reference to reports of 'your Lordship's living so beneath your quality, out of the way, and declining Court attendance', and also to the lady in question, Betty Becke, as being described by some as 'a common courtizan'. This bold and at the same time tactful letter was prompted no doubt partly by concern for his patron's welfare, and partly, it may be supposed, by a desire to check circumstances which might lead indirectly to the further deterioration of his credit, in a double sense. Sandwich almost immediately moved from Chelsea; but his treatment of Pepys for some months afterwards was cool and discouraging. The momentous letter was justified by Pepys on the ground of his sense of duty to his patron—'the duty which every bit of bread I eat tells me I owe to your Lordship'. We may wonder if, in the circumstances of the next three years, he remembered these words.

A year or so later, by which time the old cordial relationship had been restored, Sandwich went to sea, in a naval command. There was a chance that he might be killed; and Pepys naturally felt intensely anxious about his money. He managed to arrange for the repayment of £443 of the debt due to him; and a little while after, by the exercise of diplomacy, for the escape from his liability in the suretyship for £1,000. Sandwich showed no immediate signs of feeling hurt or annoyed by this apparent failure in confidence. As a result of this transaction, Pepys remarked: 'I am to my extra-ordinary comfort eased of a liablenesse to pay the sum in case of my Lord's death, or troubles in estate, or my Lord's greater fall, which God defend!' He had additional ground for anxiety on Sandwich's return from sea in the autumn of 1665. His patron's financial reputation was in risk of being adversely affected owing to his ill-considered authorization of premature distributions of captured prize goods of considerable value. Some of these, amounting, it was said, to £2,000 or more, he distributed to himself. His action was undoubtedly irregular; and he suffered in esteem accordingly.

In this trouble, Sandwich had the favour and protection of the King, who soon arranged to appoint him ambassador to Spain, and thus to have a period of respite from the imputations and accusa-tions of his enemies. Pepys, during the few weeks before his patron left for Madrid, tried to demonstrate his loyalty, but at the same time admitted to himself that he did not wish to be seen to be very closely associated with the man with whom the Duke of York was displeased about the distribution of prize goods. On Pepys asking Sandwich when and where he could wait on him, Sandwich suggested secrecy, which Pepys 'liked very well'. The next day, however, he showed a better spirit. Sandwich came late to a Council meeting presided over by the Duke of York. He looked melancholy; and there was no seat for him. Pepys rose and gave up his seat. This was doubtless interpreted as a loyal gesture; and it was intended as such.

Sandwich had not been long resident in Spain when, in 1666, he made a request to Pepys, through his steward at home, for a loan of £500. His predicament was evidently the result of extravagant expenditure. Pepys could not face what seemed to him to be a strong likelihood of the loss of so considerable a sum of money. He remarked about this request: 'I avoyded it, being not willing to embark myself in money there, where I see things going to ruine.' This was an important decision to make, for it implied a lack of trust, a lack

of friendliness, and perhaps a lack of gratitude. It is at least arguable
that, both from a prudential and an ethical point of view, he would
have been well advised to lend the money. He had by this time
raised his private fortune to about £6,000.

As Sandwich had left England with his reputation under a cloud,
and in an obviously wretched state of mind, it would seem to have
been natural and sensible for Pepys to have written him letters from
time to time to prove that, in spite of what others might do,
he remained a faithful supporter. Nearly a year passed; and he
confessed that it was a burden on his mind that he had written no
letter. His refusal to make a loan certainly rendered writing more
difficult for him. After several more months, and the arrival of a
commissary from Sandwich, Pepys's conscience was again stirred,
and more painfully. 'I was almost ashamed to see him, lest he should
know that I have not yet wrote one letter to my Lord since his
going.' A few weeks afterwards he asserted that he was in the
process of writing; and he wrote a long letter to his patron on the
7th October 1667, in which he alleged that he had addressed two
earlier letters to Spain, which, he remarked, seemed to have mis-
carried. This allegation does not agree with his statements in the
Diary, mentioned above.

At the end of 1667, Sandwich, whose extravagant expenditure
had evidently continued, was again badly in need of money; and
his elder son, Lord Hinchingbroke, was also short of funds, in
England. Pepys thereupon promised, 'much against my will', a
loan of £200 to Hinchingbroke and £60 towards answering a bill of
exchange of Lord Sandwich. A little later he promised a loan of £100
to Lady Sandwich, 'much against my will, for I fear it is as good as
lost'. By this time Sandwich was preparing to return to England. 'I
did receive another letter from my Lord Sandwich, which troubles
me to see how I have neglected him, in not writing, but once, all
this time of his being abroad; and I see he takes notice, but yet
gently, of it, that puts me to great trouble, and I know not how to
get out of it, having no good excuse, and too late now to mend, he
being coming home.'

Just before Sandwich's arrival in this country his sons told Pepys that their father would wish to borrow £500 from him. He felt that his duty to his patron required him to do 'something extraordinary in this, and the rather because I have been remiss in writing to him during this voyage, more than ever I did in my life, and more indeed than was fit for me'. He accordingly wrote a letter to Sandwich, to meet him on his arrival, offering the loan of £500; and he added, as a postscript: 'The ill state of my eyes has not allowed me to read or write thus much for several months, but by the help of another's, which, I hope, will excuse me to your Lordship, in my not appearing with my own hand here.' This lame and unconvincing excuse was doubtless intended to have a retroactive effect; but he would have done better to have been more frank.

On Sandwich's return to England, Pepys found good reason to suppose that he had been supplanted by others in his patron's confidence and affections, especially by Charles Harbord. He was given a dubious welcome when he called. He tried to persuade himself that Sandwich was in one of his unsociable moods. 'I to visit Lord Sandwich, who is now so reserved, or moped rather, I think, with his own business, that he bids welcome to no man, I think, to his satisfaction. However, I bear with it, being willing to give him as little trouble as I can, and to receive as little from him, wishing only that I had my money in my purse that I have lent him; but, however, I shew no discontent at all.'

It soon became clear that there would not be a renewal of the earlier kindnesses, though, a few months later, there was some return to the old confidence. When, in due course, Lord Sandwich made his will he did not include Pepys among his executors, nor did he leave him any remembrance. A settlement of accounts was arranged in 1670; the loan of £500 was repaid; and thereafter Lord Sandwich did not owe him any money. This sad conclusion to what was at one time a happy relationship must have distressed Pepys; and he doubtless wished that, in some respects at least, he had managed matters more judiciously.

In several instances Pepys showed himself to be fully conscious of the need to be loyal to those who had contributed to his success in his profession. He may have learnt from experience. In 1669, Sir

William Coventry, to whom he owed much for the good reputation he had with the Duke of York, was in disgrace with the King, and was imprisoned in the Tower of London, owing to his having indiscreetly challenged the Duke of Buckingham, the King's favourite, to a duel. Pepys, almost ostentatiously, made a number of visits to Coventry in the Tower, and probably ran some risks of losing Royal favour by doing so. But a little later he found it difficult to sustain this nobility of behaviour. He recorded a significant incident soon after Coventry was released from prison. 'After much discourse with him, I walked out with him into St. James's Park, where, being afeared to be seen with him, he having not yet leave to kiss the King's hand, but notice taken, as I hear, of all that go to him, I did take pretence of my attending the Tangier Committee, to take my leave, though to serve him I should, I think, stick at nothing.'

Pepys's unshakeable loyalty to the Duke of York is so well established that it requires no emphasis. The strongest instances occurred after the end of the period of the Diary. But there were early examples of his loyalty being convincingly expressed. The continuance of Pepys in office was threatened at a critical moment by the designs of the Duke of Buckingham's faction. 'I have not a mind indeed at this time', wrote Pepys, 'to be put out of my Office, if I can make any shift that is honourable to keep it, but I will not do it by deserting the Duke of York.' Ten years afterwards he was defending the Duke against violent hostility in the House of Commons; and he suffered grievously as a result.

In 1668, Pepys's colleague, Lord Brouncker, who had at an earlier date maintained very friendly relations with him, but who had lately been opposed to him on some office matters, was in bad odour in Parliamentary circles, being in risk of disgrace. Pepys had some excuse for taking care not to be seen with him. But he felt that Brouncker was being unfairly treated, and therefore walked with him publicly in Westminster Hall for a whole morning. This was the act of a manly and true-hearted friend.

The intricate personal relations between Pepys and those of his superiors who were in opposing camps have to be to some extent understood if the Diary is to yield its full meaning. Sandwich and Carteret were in one camp, and Coventry, supported by the Duke of York, was in another. Pepys had to play an artful game so as to maintain good relations with all of them. As he became more established in his office, and gained in importance, he had sometimes to choose between exhibiting an unequivocal devotion to the service of the Duke of York and paying due attention to the wishes of Lord Sandwich. The former was apt to appear the wiser choice.

It was sometimes difficult enough for Pepys to maintain his loyalty to a patron in circumstances where constancy would be to his disadvantage. But it was more difficult still when he had two supporters who were at enmity. He might easily lose the aid of one of them. For a number of years he had a most delicate role to sustain, in keeping on good terms with both Carteret and Coventry, who were strongly hostile to each other and apparently irreconcilable. Both of them were frequently useful in exercising their influence on his behalf. The situation was complicated, because failure to keep on good terms with Carteret might mean estrangement with Sandwich; and loss of support from Coventry might deprive him of the valuable favour of the Lord High Admiral. It was a matter of extreme dexterity to remain friends with both sides. At a most critical moment in this supreme balancing feat, Pepys wrote: 'Lord! to see in what difficulty I stand, that dare not walk with Sir W. Coventry, for fear my Lord or Sir G. Carteret should see me, nor with either of them, for fear Sir W. Coventry should.'

When Sandwich was about to leave England on his embassy to Spain he did not feel satisfied that Pepys was being sufficiently helpful to Carteret. He spoke to Pepys of the 'inconveniences', that is to say practical disadvantages, he might suffer if he did not fall in with Sandwich's wishes. This sounded like a threat. But Pepys evidently felt that he could manage to keep a foot in both camps, especially as Sandwich would shortly be out of the country for a considerable period. He accordingly contented himself with asking Sandwich to recognize that he had 'a very hard game to play'. A fortnight later, just before Sandwich's departure, Pepys again expressed his regret about the need for his ambiguous allegiance.

He desired that he might be considered as remaining neutral, which Sandwich 'approved and confessed reasonable, but desired me to befriend him [Carteret] privately'.

Strangely enough, Pepys, almost immediately afterwards, felt apprehensive that he might have failed to keep himself sufficiently in Coventry's good books. He therefore took advantage of a long talk with him to assure him that he was not allying himself with Carteret in a way which would imply any lack of gratitude or fidelity to him. Serving two masters was proving a perplexing and precarious business.

After Sandwich returned to England from his ambassadorship in Spain, lasting more than eighteen months, Pepys's need for extreme diplomacy in these personal relations not only remained but was intensified. Sandwich tried to induce the Duke of York to procure the appointment of a Treasurer's post at Tangier for Sir Charles Harbord, a person to whom Pepys had some reason to be ill disposed. The Duke of York had by this time a high appreciation of Pepys's value. Pepys learnt that the Duke had remarked that 'it was fit to have Mr. Pepys satisfied therein [about the proposed appointment] first', which was reasonable and proper, since Pepys was the Treasurer of the Tangier Commission. Sandwich discussed the matter with Pepys, and 'did seem industrious to let me see that he was glad that the Duke of York and he might come to contend who shall be the kindest to me, which I owned as his great love, and so I hope and believe it is, though my Lord did go a little too far in this business to move it so far, without consulting me. But I took no notice of that, but was glad to see this competition come about, that my Lord Sandwich is apparently jealous of my thinking that the Duke of York do mean me more kindness than him.' Three days afterwards Pepys, acting with discretion, announced at a Committee meeting of the Tangier Commission that he did not want to exercise his influence in the matter. Although he did not then realize how much of Sandwich's esteem he had lost, he displayed a high degree of shrewdness and tact in this and other conjunctures. These qualities were increasingly noticeable in him as his career advanced.

6

Delicate Problems

When Pepys got well into his stride at the office he not only discovered that the spur of ambition gave him a pleasurable sensation, but it became increasingly clear that, if he were to be able to live in a manner requisite to his aims, he must find means of supplementing his salary. Keeping pace with, or perhaps outstripping, the style of living maintained by his colleagues would require more than three or four hundred pounds a year. He had also to bear in mind that the times were uncertain. Even relatively minor officials could find themselves suddenly without employment, so that it was no more than prudent to build up an estate which could provide a sufficient income for at least a temporary retirement.

At the time of his appointment to the Navy Board his fortune, if it can be so described, was no more than about £150. At first he had considerable expenses in setting up house in his official quarters. He spent freely on pleasure. And, apart from the fees gained from a temporary additional post at the Privy Seal Office, he secured little in the way of extra emoluments. For the first three years in office his estate increased slowly, and it remained well short of the £1,000 mark to which he eagerly aspired. His failure to do better was not due to lack of effort. He was a novice; and he naturally found it difficult to discover the technique by which irregular profits could be obtained. Moreover, a certain standing and proficiency in his profession had to be reached. The right contacts had to be established. All this took time.

From the early days of his appointment, presents in kind flowed in. Captains of ships would express acknowledgement for favours— a few dozen of wine, or a cask of ale; something brought from abroad, a bird, a jar of olives, or a Turkey carpet. Five brace of duck were a welcome relief to the housekeeping account. Christmas presents from naval officers, dockyard officials, and contractors were quite permissible if they consisted merely of 'a great chine of beef' or 'four great turkies'. Though very welcome, gifts of this kind did little to solve Pepys's pecuniary problems.

By 1664 contractors who wished to secure contracts through Pepys's good offices gave him valuable presents of silver articles, such as 'state cups', and sets of candlesticks. At this stage his profits from victualling contracts amounted to some hundreds of pounds a year. This increase in scale was most gratifying and satisfactory; but it involved some misgivings, both practical and, to a less extent, moral. There were risks that an ill-affected person would discover the facts and report them to someone who might initiate action of an unpleasant kind. There began to be much public talk about bribery and corruption in the middle period of the Diary; and Commissioners of Accounts set up by Parliament, as well as a Committee of Accounts, were penetrating in their inquiries, and caused Pepys a good deal of anxiety lest some of his transactions with contractors should be disclosed. The attempts of the Commissioners of Accounts to uncover his acceptance of bribes from Sir W. Warren in respect of contracts for timber were particularly vexatious.

It must always be remembered, when considering Pepys's conduct in the acceptance of bribes, that bribery was condoned by many eminent persons, especially if it was not unreasonable in extent. If an official arranged a contract so that the price was fair and the quality of the goods unimpeachable, it was not thought improper if a moderate sum was paid to him by the contractor. Pepys frequently laid down certain basic principles on this subject. He considered it reprehensible, or at least dangerous, for a public servant to accept money from a contractor on condition that he favoured him. It was different if the official had, of his own free will, done a favour which in no way imperilled the public interest, and subsequently received payment by way of acknowledgement. But it was, of course, extremely difficult to distinguish between these two procedures in practice. The *ex post facto* voluntary payment may have been an implied term in the original transaction, though a pretence was maintained that the contractor was free from obligation. If this plan was adopted, the ultimate payment was in fact safe, for the contractor knew that, if he did not pay, he would never be given another contract by the disappointed official.

This was the situation when Edward Deering sold to the Navy, through the instrumentality of Pepys, some timber that he had on his hands and wanted to get rid of. At the beginning of the negotiations between Pepys and Deering's representative Pepys asserted that 'as I would not by any thing be bribed to be unjust in my dealings, so I was not so squeamish as not to take people's acknowledgment where I had the good fortune by my pains to do them good and just offices, and so I would not come to be at any agreement with him, but I would labour to do him this service and to expect his consideration thereof afterwards as he thought fit'. He received £50 in due course. This was not quite as much as he had hoped, but he was satisfied. His evasion of the difficulty, in regard to a later contract with Deering, is described in delightfully naïve terms. He was offered twenty pieces of gold to arrange the affair, and he refused, 'resolving not to be bribed to dispatch business, but will have it done however out of hand forthwith'. In other words, he would not take money as a condition precedent, but he would quickly put the contract through, knowing full well that he would receive the twenty pieces in due course.

Sometimes the contractors, instead of paying a generous lump sum of money to the official, paid him a percentage of his profits resulting from a contract. For instance, Pepys enabled a Captain Grove to have the business of hiring ships for Tangier, and it was well understood that he should have a percentage of the profits so gained. Similar arrangements were made in some of the contracts with Warren for the supply of timber, and with others in regard to victualling.

In the earlier stages of his business relations with Warren he received presents of money after, and not before, contracts had been concluded. But even these *ex post facto* payments were treated by both of them as matters of extreme secrecy. On one occasion Warren had given Pepys to understand that he would pay £100 if two large contracts for masts went through. When the time for payment came they repaired to a tavern and, 'being all alone', a bag with the money in it changed hands. No written record of the transaction was kept.

There were one or two instances in which Pepys could not resist accepting a bribe as a condition precedent to the contract. In these circumstances an elaborate pretence had to be staged, so that the bribe was presumed to be an expression of admiration or good-will, or else the acknowledgement of some imaginary kindness in the past. For example, Gauden, a prominent victualling contractor, wished to engage Pepys's help in securing a large contract; and he asked Pepys to accept two very large and valuable silver flagons, worth about £100. Pepys knew full well Gauden's object, and that an acceptance of this tempting gift was contrary to his principles. He could not, however, resist the allurement of seeing his cupboard of plate enriched by these sumptuous objects. But matters could not be left like that. The danger was too great. So, a little later, he managed to obtain an assurance from Gauden that, although he would much value Pepys's helpfulness in regard to the proposed contract, 'what he did [in giving the flagons] was for my old kindnesses to him in dispatching his business, which I was glad to hear, and with my heart in good rest and great joy parted, and to my business again'. He could now keep the flagons in his cupboard, and enjoy their magnificence without uncomfortable apprehensions, for he had an adequate answer to any impertinent questioner.

The same kind of farce was enacted with Captain Beckford, a contractor in seamen's clothing, who presented Pepys with 'a little purse with gold in it', expressed to be an acknowledgement of past favours. Pepys protested that there had been none, but, on pressure, accepted the purse, 'and so fell to talk of his business', that is to say to make preparations for entering into a contract. It was tacitly understood between them that the acceptance of the purse implied Pepys's help; but care was taken not to admit this in words. Pepys, however, was not quite happy about his behaviour on this occasion. 'I was not fully justified in my taking it, because of my submitting myself to the having it objected against me hereafter . . .' Doubtless, on these occasions, satisfactory reliance was placed on expressive looks and grimaces. These were as effective as words, for it was to the official's interest to keep on good terms with open-handed contractors.

Other stratagems were adopted by Pepys with the object of approximating to the principles he had laid down for himself, and thus ensuring his safety from the clutches of the law. Once, when he was dealing with contractors whom he suspected might prove unreliable, he would only accept the money through a third party, a middle-man; and he made it a further condition that he should not be required to express any thanks to the principals or make any acknowledgement of the money received.

Perhaps the most ridiculous attempt to protect himself, and possibly to ease his conscience at the same time, was in relation to the Captain Grove above-mentioned and the hiring of ships for Tangier. 'I met Captain Grove,' he said, 'who did give me a letter directed to myself from himself. I discerned money to be in it, and took it, knowing, as I found it to be, the proceeds of the place I have got him to be, the taking up of vessels for Tangier. But I did not open it till I came home to my office, and there broke it open, not looking into it till all the money was out, that I might say I saw no money in the paper, if ever I should be questioned about it. There was a piece of gold and £4 in silver.' He can hardly have believed that this childish expedient could be in any way a source of protection. He might, with equal expectation of immunity from risk of pains and penalties, have alleged that he had received the money as a present from his fairy godmother. A slightly more promising opportunity for dissembling presented itself when a parcel included both a gift of gloves for Mrs. Pepys and money for Pepys. Here, if questioned, he could remember the gloves and forget the money.

The device whereby contractors gave presents to Mrs. Pepys rather than to Pepys was occasionally used; and it had its obvious advantages. But it was not practicable when considerable sums were involved.

Time and again Pepys insisted that he would not take any bribe that had the result of making the transaction one by which the interest of the King's service suffered. In his first large contract with Warren for £3,000 worth of masts he concluded his comments by remarking: 'But I hope my pains was such, as the King has the best bargain of masts has been bought these 27 years in this office.' He had to prove to the Navy Board, and especially to some very critical members of it, the benefits of both price and quality in regard to a later contract with Warren: 'I was very hard with him, even to the making him angry, but I thought it fit to do it as well as just for my owne [and] the King's behalf.' In contracts for tar and canvas: 'I held them [the contractors] to some terms against their wills, to the King's advantage.'

Sometimes his insistence on his moral rectitude may appear a little excessive; but, in the main, he doubtless adhered to this essential principle. In a contract with Deering, he alleged: 'I do really believe that I did what is to the King's advantage in it.' And, at a later stage, he stated that 'there is not the least word or deed I have yet been guilty of in his behalf but what I am sure has been to the King's advantage and the profit of the service, nor ever will'.

In his record of his arrangements with two contractors for the victualling of the garrison of Tangier, Allsopp and Lanyon, he observed: 'I hope I may get nobly and honestly with profit to the king.' And, later, when he had received £105, his first profit on the victualling of Tangier, he alleged that he had so ordered matters that he would save the King £5,000 per annum 'and yet get myself a hope of £300 per annum without the least wrong to the King'. But he seems to have admitted that he had accepted the contractors' prices of all provisions without due investigation; and, when, some time afterwards, it was suggested to him by his supposed friend Creed that these contractors were being overpaid, he noted that this was a matter 'which I was formerly aware of, but did wink at'. Pepys was worried by this suggestion of Creed's, but concluded by thinking that 'no harm will arise thereby'. Perhaps these transactions might have involved anyone less adroit in serious trouble.

In respect of one commodity, calico for flags, Pepys was exceptionally rash. He decided that he would purchase calico himself and sell it to the Navy Board at a profit. In this transaction he was acting in two inconsistent capacities; and it need hardly be said that this kind of activity was illegal. He bought 200 pieces of calico at a cost of about £500, 'and as I know I shall save the King money, so I hope to get a little for my pains and venture of my own money myself'. A few months later he made a profit of 'at least £50' on the deal, and alleged that he had saved the King 'near £100'. He managed to get this account passed for payment by his friendly colleague, Carteret, who was Treasurer. But a year or so later Parliament was in hot pursuit of any irregularities of this kind in naval administration. Pepys happened one day to be at Carteret's lodgings, 'and there looking over the book that Sir G. Carteret intends to deliver to the Parliament of his payments since September 1st, 1664, and there I find my name the very second [in order] for flags, which I had bought for the Navy, of calico, once, about 500 and odd pounds, which vexed me mightily. At last, I concluded of scraping out my name and putting in Mr. Tooker's [a messenger to the Navy Commissioners] which eased me; though the price was such as I should have had glory by.' Even this rash expedient did not prevent ultimate disclosure; and the matter was investigated by the Commissioners of Accounts. But Pepys's culpability was not, it seems, pressed, it being regarded as a single incident where urgency and necessity could be claimed as justification, as well as alleged financial benefit to the King. Pepys's ingenuity evidently extricated him from a very awkward situation.

There seems to be only one occasion recorded in the Diary in which Pepys refused to accept a proffered gift of money from aspiring contractors. It was at a time when Parliament had ordered strenuous investigations into bribery, corruption, and profit-making by departmental officials. Two contractors for the supply of flags 'with mighty earnestness did present me with, and press me to take a box, wherein I could not guess there was less than £100 in gold; but I do wholly refuse it, and did not at last take it. The truth is, not thinking them safe men to receive such a gratuity from, nor knowing any considerable courtesy that ever I did to them, but desirous to keep myself free from their reports, and to have it in my power to say I had refused their offer.' Pepys was doubtless right to decide as he did, from every point of view. If, as was not unlikely, he should find himself in an unpleasant predicament before a committee of accounts in regard to some other transaction, he could support his insistence on his innocence by citing this refusal.

A similar instinctive sense of caution operated in his dealings with Warren. He broke off friendly relations with him, after some years of mutually profitable co-operation, on scenting danger. Warren had begun to court another member of the Navy Board, Lord Brouncker; and Pepys surmised that it would be prudent to terminate his partnership with Warren. This course was perhaps all the more advisable because Brouncker, who seems not to have been well off, was inclined to look askance at Pepys's sudden increase in fortune. He felt that he could not trust Warren as he used to do, 'for I will not be inward with him that is open to another'.

Although Pepys often took bribes, and made profits from contracts, he was determined that the principle that the King's interest must be paramount should extend to the general practice of the Navy Board. He took active steps to discover which contractors would charge the lowest prices. He went to Thames Street, for instance, 'and there enquired among the shops the price of tarre and oyle, and do find great content in it, and hope to save the King money by this practice'. Soon after this he tried to induce the Navy Board to standardize this procedure. They 'met several tradesmen by appointment to know of them their lowest rates that they sell to us, for I resolve to know that, and to buy no dearer, that so when we know the lowest rate, it shall be the Treasurer's fault, and not ours, that we pay dearer'. He was obviously aiming at the prevention of hole-in-the-corner contracts arranged by single members of the Board at inflated prices, where large presents from the contractors would naturally be involved. His attempt to introduce this reform proves that he was serious in his declaration that the King's interest must always be the first consideration.

When, after the end of the period of the Diary, Pepys was appointed Secretary of the Admiralty, he seems to have taken but few bribes. It may well be that, by this time, he considered that he had accumulated a sufficient estate for his needs. Or, more likely, increasing experience impressed him with the need for a higher degree of circumspection. After returning from his sojourn in France in 1669, he thought it possible that he might have to defend himself against charges of accepting bribes. The Commissioners of Accounts were then very active in such matters. Accordingly, he wrote an elaborate letter to them exculpating himself. In this letter he not only denied ever asking for or accepting money to the detriment of the King's service, but he also alleged that his profits from his appointment during the ten years that he had been in office amounted to quite a small figure. 'I find not', he said, 'my estate at this day bettered by one thousand pounds, from all the profits, salary, and other advantages arising from the said employment, beyond what it was known to be at my admission thereto.' He had stated in the Diary that he began his career in the administration of the Navy with about £150; and, by the end of 1669, he must have been worth at least £9,000. When, therefore, he penned the above-quoted self-justification, he was prevaricating in a defiant and reckless manner.

His alarming experience, of being in danger of having his indiscretions exposed and punished, doubtless gave him cause to ponder. He became increasingly aware of the risks of discovery; and he realized that, if discovered, he would probably be incapacitated from his continued devotion to the object that meant more to him than any other, the efficiency of the Navy.

7

Getting and Spending

Where money was concerned, as in many other matters, Pepys's behaviour seems to lack consistency. He was fond of money in the sense that he was constantly concerned in putting it by so as to accumulate a sizeable fortune. The main object of this habit of saving was to make himself secure against adversity, and, incidentally, if there was no adversity, to sustain the steady advancement in rank and prestige that he desired. He tried to be careful and prudent in his disbursements. But, as he grew more prosperous, he was often such a lavish spender that he cannot be described as parsimonious.

It is understandable that, in his early stages as a capitalist, he disliked parting with money as much as he enjoyed amassing it. At a time when his whole savings had amounted to no more than about £250, and he was still engaged in setting up house in his official quarters, a friend of his whom he valued highly, and whom he thought 'honest and sufficient', was in great need of a loan of £200. He was inclined to blame himself because' lothness to part with money did dissuade me from it'. But it is doubtful if he can be blamed. More than a year afterwards a little money meant a lot to him. When he paid his teacher of musical composition a fee of £5 he remarked that it was 'a great deal of money and troubled me to part with it'.

He could, however, rise above temptations to undue acquisitiveness, and could adopt an open-handed alternative. When his finances were still very slender he lent his father £6. His father, though far from being well off, soon offered to repay the loan, 'but, it went against me to take it of him, and therefore I did not, though I was afterwards a little troubled that I did not'. This incident well illustrates the way in which he was sometimes pulled in two different directions at the same time in regard to money.

After a year in office, with only £350 a year for salary, plus a few extras and perquisites, his savings had only risen a small extent. He began to be 'more and more thoughtful about getting money than ever heretofore'. 'I hope', he said, 'to find out some job or other that I may get a sum by to set me up.' This topic kept recurring during the next two or three years. In 1662 he consulted with his friend Creed about money-making, 'which I am now giving myself wholly up to . . .' But, during that year he improved his total no more than from £500 to £650; and, at the end of 1663, only to £800. By 1664 he had made some useful friends, and had gained some valuable information about ways of obtaining larger perquisites. Money began to come in rapidly. Yet he felt more strongly than ever about the need for building up a fortune. He noted: '. . . my head at this juncture was full of business how to get something.' When at the end of 1664 he had attained to a figure of £1,349, he declared: 'The Lord make me ever thankful to his holy name for it!' This was not an isolated outburst, for after he had advanced to the impressive total of £6,200 at the end of 1666, chiefly as a result of larger presents and profits from contractors, he regarded the accomplishment as one 'for which the Holy Name of God be praised!'

When expenditure was in respect of an object which would give him pleasure, he did not stint it. As soon as he took possession of his official residence he determined to make it a source of pride and satisfaction. He undertook re-decorations and improvements, and purchased new fittings and furniture. The dining-room was 'finished with green serge hanging and gilt leather which is very handsome'. (Later, it was wainscoted.) Parts of his parlour were gilded. New fireplaces were installed, with handsome overmantels. Pewter sconces adorned the entry and stairway. In the summer of

1662 the house was raised by an extra story; and this involved further expenditure in decoration and furniture. Although his standards were high, a great deal of this outlay was unavoidable. And he could remind himself that there was no rent to pay.

He appreciated that handsome rooms, elegant contents, and a stylish manner of entertainment would not only improve his self-esteem, but were important in raising his status and enhancing his value in his profession. For these reasons, he spent a considerable amount of money on table silver, including dishes and ornaments; and, after some years, he bought silver plates so that, on special occasions, his guests might not have to eat off anything less lordly. When remarking on the first dinner-party at which the silver plates were used, he said: 'I did make them all gaze to see themselves served so nobly in plate, and a neat dinner, indeed, though but of seven dishes.' When writing again on the same subject, he expressed his enjoyment in having 'all things rich and handsome about me'. He had the tastes of the aristocracy.

When he gave a grand dinner-party he was liberal in expenditure, even at the stage at which his income was still very moderate. He reckoned that three dinners, given in quick succession in 1661, had together cost him £15. There was no skimping on that scale. About £5 seems to have been the normal amount for him to pay for a dinner with eight guests. Six or seven 'noble dishes', with a specially imported male cook in charge, were served on such occasions. His most expensive dinner-party, towards the end of the period of the Diary, cost about £12. His standard of entertainment had to be as good as, or better than, that of anyone else of similar rank and station. He despised a stingy host; and was never tired of jeering at the miserable menus at Sir William Penn's.

He did not hesitate to indulge his personal tastes, and spent a good deal of money on buying books, and having them bound or re-bound. Ten pounds and more were spent in a year on these objects. Perhaps £5 or so on musical instruments. A microscope cost him £5. 10s. 0d. Pictures of his wife and himself were freely commissioned. His own portrait was painted by Savill and by Hales, and later by Lely and Kneller. His wife's, by Hales, cost £14; and a miniature of her by Samuel Cooper cost £30, plus £8. 3s. 4d. for the case, etc. In making up his accounts for 1664, the first year in which his income rose rapidly, he spent £420; in 1665 £509; and, at the end of 1666, he found that he had spent as much as £1,154 during that year, more than twice the amount of his expenditure in the previous year. He was shocked at his extravagance; but he could afford it, for, as we have just seen, his income had recently increased by leaps and bounds.

It is difficult to understand how he can have spent as much as he did in 1666. He mentioned, as examples of large outlays during the year, £80 for a necklace for his wife, £40 for a new set of chairs and couch, and nearly £40 for three pictures. But even these only total £160; and he did not appear to spend a great deal on clothes in that year. Whatever the particulars may have been, this lavishness is a conclusive reply to anyone who might suggest that he was miserly and close-fisted. If he set his heart on an item of expenditure, counsels of financial prudence were irrelevant. He saw a copper cistern for the table which attracted him. He learnt that it would cost £6 or £7; 'but', he remarked peremptorily, 'I will have one'. This was much in the same spirit that he wrote about a new kind of organ that took his fancy (p. 62 below).

His greatest extravagance, perhaps, was dress. He evidently decided from the time of his appointment to the Navy Board that his clothes must be more respectable than hitherto. In early days he felt rash in ordering 'a fine camlett cloak with gold buttons' and a silk suit. 'I pray God to make me able to pay for it.' This was the first silk suit he had ever had. A velvet coat ordered in the same year, with a jackanapes coat with silver buttons, strained his finances considerably. He had little money to spare during these early years, but he could not resist a 'slasht doublet', and a beaver hat, costing as much as £4. 5s. 0d. These articles were doubtless good of their kind, but they were not adequate to his aspirations. Towards the end of 1663 he decided that economy in clothes was bad policy; and 'having considered with my wife very much of the inconveniences of my going in no better plight, we did resolve of putting me into a better garb, and, among other things, to have a good velvet cloak; that is, of cloth lined with velvet and other things modish, and a perruque . . .' He concluded that an ample outlay on fine clothes might well bring in a comparable return, 'for I perceive how I have hitherto suffered for lack of going as becomes my place'; and he hoped that he would have opportunities for getting more money 'than when, for want of clothes, I was forced to sneake like a beggar'. As a result of these deliberations, he spent £55 on clothes for himself and about £12 on his wife. His own new clothes included the velvet cloak, a purple shag gown trimmed with gold buttons and twist, a black cloth suit trimmed with scarlet ribbon, and 'silk tops for my legs' (described elsewhere in the Diary as 'black silk knit canons'), also two periwigs costing £5.

From this time onwards he maintained his contention that a rich appearance paid. In the next year he said: 'I find that I must go handsomely, whatever it costs me, and the charge will be made up in the fruit it brings.' He proceeded to buy 'a dear and noble suit costing me about £17'. This was a period when contractors of various types were calling at the office to try and arrange deals, and were looking for a suitable official, one who would carry weight. If he seemed to be prosperous, he would be taken to be an influential member of the Board, and might well be chosen as the best man with whom to do business. If he was chosen, he would have a good chance of making money.

How far vanity entered into Pepys's growing expenditure on clothes is a matter for conjecture. It is, however, clear from several descriptions of his attendances at church on Sundays, wearing his latest handsome clothes, that he dearly loved to 'cut a dash' and catch the admiring eyes of his fellow parishioners. His standard of modish dress grew higher and higher. It was at his wife's dictation, he said, that he acquired a new silk camelot suit, very rich and noble, costing more than £24. He also ordered a coat trimmed with gold buttons with broad gold lace on the cuffs. Instead of his 'little sword, with gilt handle', he began to wear a new silver-hilted sword. 'I like myself mightily in it, and so do my wife.' To these glories, he added a new periwig; and, with this and a new suit, he made 'a great shew' in church. Next, he delighted in tunics of velvet, laced with silk lace, and 'a flowered tabby vest'.

Towards the end of the period of the Diary he was apt to indulge in lavish expenditure if some pleasing object caught his eye. He had desired some rich embellishment of his study, and paid £83 for a set of tapestry hangings for it. The height of aggrandizement, exceeding perhaps the limits of discretion, was reached when, in 1669, he purchased a coach and horses and drove out apparelled in an expensive suit with much gold lace on the sleeves. It was hinted to him that this behaviour was likely to arouse unwelcome comment; and he accordingly decided to have the gold lace removed.

The acquisition of a well-designed, stylish coach and a fine pair of horses marked the summit of his ambition in the way of outward show. He had reached the stage when he was 'almost ashamed to be seen in a hackney', 'for I do see that my condition do require it [a coach], as well as that it is more charge to my purse to live as I do [hiring hackney coaches] than keep one'. One day, in May 1669, when he was wearing his gold-laced sleeves, 'we went alone through the town with our new liveries of serge, and the horses' manes and tails tied with red ribbons, and the standards there gilt with varnish, and all clean, and green reines, that people did mightily look upon us; and the truth is, I did not see any coach more pretty, though more gay, than ours, all the day'. It was a notable success in social advancement, to which he had attained after only a few years in office. But in such a triumph there were pitfalls lurking. He heard that his lordly equipage had been remarked upon, and that people were evidently wondering what was the source of all this wealth. It occurred to him that this sumptuous display might provoke inconvenient questioning. Committees were still inquiring into irregularities in naval administration. He could accuse himself of some rashness in this ostentatious expenditure when there were, he had heard, powerful influences at work plotting his removal from office.

Much as he loved money, he could not be a miser, for he had an immense capacity for enjoyment; and enjoyment often means spending. Most of his expenditure gave him keen pleasure, especially that devoted to hospitality and the provision of entertainment for his friends. He was fundamentally sociable. After a long evening of varied amusement, with dancing accompanied by four fiddlers, singing of many kinds, 'things of three voices', Irish, Italian, and other solos, he was 'mightily' satisfied, 'thinking it to be one of the merriest enjoyment I must look for in the world, and did content myself therefore with the thoughts of it, and so to bed; only [he added characteristically] the musique did not please me, they not being contented with less than 30s.'

He occasionally philosophized about the justifications of pleasure. Enjoyment was, he considered, the aim and object of life; it was 'the height of what we take pains for and can hope for in this world'. He regarded it as 'the greatest real comfort that I am to expect in the world, and that it is that we do really labour in the hopes of'. We may not agree with this generalization without some qualification; but it can help to explain some puzzling features in his behaviour.

Captious people might assert that his own enjoyment bulked to an immoderate extent in his attitude to life, and that, if he was lavish in the expenditure of money, this was primarily aimed at satisfying his own desires. In fact, his delight in giving pleasure to other people is too evident to be disputed.

8

Business and Diversions

———————◦◦◦◦———————

In whatever aspect we study Pepys's character we find complexity and contrasting features. He combined in a remarkable way capacity for strenuous activity in his professional sphere and whole-hearted indulgence in pleasure. In the main he succeeded in keeping his business and diversions in due proportion, and rarely allowed either a sense of duty to predominate unduly or siren strains to bewitch him so as to diminish his habitual diligence. Occasionally pleasure, specially exemplified in playgoing, proved too seductive. On the other hand, it is obvious from numerous entries in the Diary that he genuinely enjoyed the task of increasing his professional ability by steady application to naval pursuits. For instance: 'I having lately followed my business much, find great pleasure in it and a growing content.' And, some five years later: '. . . fell to business, and did very much with infinite joy to myself . . .'

As soon as he attained to an adequate recognition of the potentialities of his post on the Navy Board, he aimed at a full six days' work a week; and sometimes his working hours extended from early morning to late at night with but little intermission. During several summers he was frequently at his office by six or seven o'clock in the morning; sometimes earlier. He allowed himself but few and brief holidays, averaging a week or two in the year, when he generally visited his country home; and, on these occasions, private business often engaged his attention.

His energy and enterprise were evident not only in revealing dishonesty and inefficiency, and in inventing means of reducing their extent, but in introducing positive means of efficiency. He was clever at unmasking fraudulent contractors. Bad-quality hemp, he found, was being supplied for rope-making; and exorbitant prices were being charged by flag-makers. Both quality and price of timber and masts engaged his earnest attention. He introduced new book-keeping methods whereby, for instance, the cost of separate jobs could be calculated. He also invented ways of keeping statistical records. He found means by which particulars of contracts for various commodities could be entered in books so as to be comparable over a period of years.

Neatness in the filing, indexing, and orderly arrangement of correspondence, memoranda, and accounts became a matter of intense interest to him. Sets of records were bound in volumes and neatly labelled. Papers were folded and sorted. Red ink was used so as to assist easy reference. These are details at which some might scoff; but the total effect of this systematization must have enhanced the competence of administration by the Navy Board, for it cannot be doubted that, up till then, the organization of the paper-work of the office had been primitive, and even chaotic. This addiction to neatness was also markedly noticeable in his arrangement and cataloguing of his library. It seems odd that this precise, orderly man could, on occasion, be so disorderly and unbridled.

During the period of the Diary, prior, that is to say, to the stage when he was Secretary of the Admiralty, he did not have much opportunity of directly influencing naval policy. But in his later career he showed himself capable of taking effective executive decisions, and of handling urgent situations with shrewdness and alacrity. In 1673, for example, when our trading vessels were being harried by the Dutch, he quickly appreciated the need for new means of protection, and, as a result of his timely intervention, a system of convoys was introduced. As he was given more power, and as he accumulated knowledge and experience, he developed increasingly the qualities of initiative and enterprise.

His action during the most alarming stage of the Great Fire, fairly early in his career, was suggestive of his later ability for directing affairs. He alone, it seems, perceived the need for pulling down, or blowing up, houses so as to check the spread of the fire, and also had the sense to obtain without delay the King's order to the Lord Mayor for this action to be taken.

He was never lacking in the essential quality of self-confidence, being always willing to undertake responsibility. Perhaps he sometimes went a little too far; and it is arguable that the highly critical attitude he frequently adopted in regard to some of his colleagues was a natural expression of a considerable degree of complacency. But, if it is true that he now and then transgressed the line between self-confidence and self-satisfaction, this may, in his instance, be regarded as an excusable foible. He constantly disparaged the way in which the office was organized, and attributed much of the inefficiency to the lack of administrative capacity of the Comptroller of the Navy Board, Sir J. Minnes. While well aware of this weakness, Pepys considered that the trouble was mainly due to more fundamental causes, and that control was too decentralized and dispersed. Towards the end of the period of the Diary he discussed these questions with his confidential assistant, Will Hewer, and expressed the opinion 'that the best way to have it [the work of the office] well done, were to have the whole trust in one, as myself, to set whom I pleased to work in the several businesses of the office, and me to be accountable for the whole, and that would do it, as I would find the instruments . . .' Few passages in the Diary disclose so effectively Pepys's combination of discernment, enterprise, and self-confidence. Administrative problems never daunted him. He would tackle them on his own initiative, and in a positive and constructive way. And yet he had a counterbalancing streak of modesty. On more than one occasion he attributed his success as an administrator largely to his diligence, his punctuality in his dealings, and his ability to take pains.

The notable administrative capacity that he displayed so convincingly in the latter part of the period of the Diary was doubtless improved by its exercise. No one taught him: the gift was inherent. Soon after his appointment, however, he came to the realization that he could not be successful unless he acquired a good deal of technical knowledge about such subjects as shipbuilding, and the materials used for the construction, upkeep, and handling of ships of war, as well as particulars in regard to the way in which sailors were fed, clothed, and paid. His easy, sociable manner, combined with a naturally inquiring mind, helped to qualify him for the acquisition of a mass of information valuable for the proper understanding of his business, and essential in gaining, not only the respect of the dockyard officials, but the approbation of his superiors.

He started in almost complete ignorance of naval matters. But he lost no time in making a senior clerk discourse to him 'of sea terms'. At Deptford dockyard he found a captain 'to shew me every hole and corner of the ship, much to my information, and the purpose of my going'. He also arranged for a knowledgeable ship's mate to give him lectures on 'the body of a ship, which my having of a modell in the office is of great use to me, and very pleasant and useful it is'. Later, Captain (later Sir Anthony) Deane, an expert in shipbuilding, gave him valuable instruction on that subject. He spent much time in studying the qualities of timber, and learnt the process of measuring it, which proved valuable in checking possible irregularities. He delighted in the practice of measuring, learning in due course how to measure ships, a faculty by which, he judged, he might save the King money.

Hemp for ropes was a commodity in regard to which he devoted considerable energy. When visiting the rope-yard at Woolwich, he 'looked over several sorts of hemp, and did fall upon my great survey of seeing the working and experiments of the strength and the charge in the dressing of every sort; and I do think I have brought it to so great a certainty, as I have done the King great service in it . . .' A few days later he was at the rope-yard again, 'and there staid till night, repeating severall trialls of the strength, wayte, waste, and other things of hemp, by which I have furnished myself enough to finish my intended business of stating the goodness of all sorts of hemp'. Canvas for sail-making, tar for various protective purposes, anchors, and lanterns were also among the

objects of his investigation. He was by no means content to confine
his activities to the office and to paper-work. Moreover, diverse
matters which only indirectly affected his administrative duties
excited his curiosity, such as 'the course of the tides' and the
ordinary law of the land. He spent a morning 'reading some
Common Law, to which I shall allot a little time now and then'.

Inquiring rather than inquisitive, he had the scientist's belief
that miscellaneous knowledge of almost any kind can be usefully
accumulated in the mind, ready to be employed in an emergent
situation, with possibly valuable results. He was, therefore, suitably
chosen as a Fellow of the Royal Society. Several of his occasional
interests were concerned with such subjects as the science of optics
and the science of sound. He acquired a microscope, and read books
on its management and application. Sometimes he made good use of
casual meetings with experts, even those of a relatively humble
kind. An account given by the King's Falconer, regarding the
tremendous force exercised in the striking power of hawks, aroused
his keen attention. Even the humble craft of sawing marble was of
sufficient interest to cause him to stay and talk 'a great while' with
a workman, while he learnt a number of details about tools and
processes. It is by no means to his discredit that, in seeking
miscellaneous knowledge, he accepted as true some very un-
scientific stories told him both by experts and amateurs. Many
intelligent people did the same. Mr. Ashmole assured him that
frogs and many insects often fall from the sky, ready formed. Even
more extravagant was a story which he noted uncritically as 'very
strange'. Serpents, he was told, fed on larks: 'they do eject poyson
up to the bird: for the bird do suddenly come down again in its
course of a circle, and falls directly into the mouth of the serpent'.
Neither did he doubt the report that it was possible to discover
whether a woman was a 'maid' or not by watching the behaviour
of a weighted string hung near her head.

Music and playgoing apart, there was little in the way of
recreation that Pepys preferred to pleasant conversation. Even
Minnes and Batten could delight him by 'most excellent discourse
of former passages of sea commanders and officers of the navy'. He

frequently enjoyed good talk at coffee-houses, being much entertained by authoritative comments on serious subjects. Once it
happened that 'we light upon very good company and had very
good discourse concerning insects and their having a generative
faculty as well as other creatures'. The variety of subject-matter to
which he was prepared to listen is proof of his appetite for almost
any kind of information. He reported hearing discussions about
such varied subjects as Sweden and the iron trade, the resuscitation
of swallows, planting fir trees, the Roman Empire, and government
in Turkey.

Matters of topical interest by no means came amiss, such as the
doings at Court, or a condemned man's behaviour at the scaffold.
A considerable proportion of the Diary is, in fact, devoted to what
can be properly described as scandal. He had many informants about
the King's amours and about other goings-on in the royal entourage.
Pierce, the Court surgeon, Mrs. Knepp the actress, his friend Creed,
and Mrs. Sarah, of the domestic staff at Lord Sandwich's, were
among those who kept him well primed. Lady Castlemaine's
activities were constantly remarked upon—how she was always
with the King, or how the King neglected her; how the Queen was
scorned, or highly esteemed. Mrs. Stewart (afterwards Duchess of
Richmond) was alternately a lady of unimpeachable morals or the
King's new mistress. The King himself and the Duke of Buckingham were remarked as being censurable in a variety of ways.

Pepys obviously gained immense pleasure from the savouring of
these piquant trifles. Nor was he averse to listening to tittle-tattle
relating to his own acquaintances. His neighbour, Mrs. Turner,
was a great disseminator of spicy stories. In this way he learnt that
the Penns were mean-minded, even dishonest; and they were
constantly borrowing pots and pans. Lord Brouncker, she disclosed,
had another mistress, besides Mrs. Williams, and so on. There is no
denying that scandal had a fascination for Pepys; and doubtless the
entertaining quality of the Diary is improved as a consequence.

But coarseness and vulgarity in conversation were apt to disgust
him, though he was always ready for hearty merriment. Gross and
indelicate talk was particularly offensive to him. He remarked of

some rogues of his acquaintance: '. . . but Lord! their mad bawdy talk did make my heart ake!' And again, 'But Lord! what loose cursed company was this, that I was in to-night, though full of wit . . .' At a dinner he at first enjoyed the merriment, but soon grew tired of his companions, 'their discourse so free'. 'Mean' or 'shallow' discourse, 'void of method and sense', as opposed to 'noble', 'manly', or 'ingenious' discourse, was, for him, so much waste of time, and exasperating into the bargain. 'But Lord! the sorry talke and discourse among the great courtiers round about him [the King], without any reverence in the world but with so much disorder.' But gaiety he loved, often affirming his zest for it, delighting, for instance, in 'very good merry discourse at dinner'.

On many occasions he not merely contributed freely to the jollification, but was the mainspring of merriment. Indeed, he was sometimes prepared to act as the 'funny man', or even, when the situation was desperate, as the buffoon of the party. In such a conjuncture his main means of exciting mirth was to find some preposterous excuse for kissing the ladies; and, by this means, while amusing others, he regaled himself. He pretended, for instance, that it was necessary to defend the ladies from being kissed by some audacious male, and that the best way of doing this was to kiss the ladies himself. Or he would invent some story of ancient custom. A game of forfeits provided him with just the opportunities he wanted. But he could also act the fool in male company. When told, during a visit to a dockyard, that his bedroom was haunted, he, though secretly a little uneasy, pretended that he was terrified, indulging in a droll and realistic piece of acting that delighted his companions.

He took great pleasure in being the entertaining host, or the guest who is the prompter and prime mover of jollity; and he disclosed some self-satisfaction in these abilities. When describing a dinner-party which he gave to the Penns and the Battens, he remarked: '. . . very pleasant I was all day . . . and I made very good company.' But he was not likely to enjoy a dinner at the Penns unless he exerted himself to make things 'go'. 'Indifferent merry to which I contributed the most', he observed in regard to one of these parties. He gave a return dinner on the next day and was proud to outdo the Penns in every way. They were served nobly, eating from silver plates. It was a 'neat dinner'. 'Mighty merry I was, and made them all, and they mightily pleased.'

Amusement seems to have been very easily provoked in those days. Circumstances that today would be regarded as highly aggravating were treated as comical. Pepys and a friend, when on their travels, were given beds with bedclothes that were quite inadequate—'he and I very merry to find how little and thin clothes they give us to cover us, so that we were fain to lie in our stockings and drawers, and lay all our coates and clothes upon the bed'. On another journey: 'Up, finding our beds good but lousy: which made us merry.' He considered the experience of being woken up by a snoring bedfellow to be intensely amusing. While it can be assumed that many of his contemporaries would not have been so uniformly indulgent in such circumstances, Pepys was doubtless not singular in this light-hearted treatment of not inconsiderable inconveniences. They were perhaps so frequent at that period that a cheerful acceptance of the inevitable was expedient.

He must have been an exceptionally energetic, indeed quite tireless, host at a party. While he was enjoying himself at the play one afternoon, his home and office were being prepared for a special evening's jollification to which a number of guests had been invited. At first, there was dancing accompanied by the music of four players. 'By and by to my house, to a very good supper, and mighty merry, and good musick playing; and after supper to dancing and singing till about twelve at night; and then we had a good sack posset for them, and an excellent cake. . . . And so to dancing again, and singing, with extraordinary great pleasure, till about two in the morning, and then broke up . . .' Needless to say, he only gave parties of these dimensions at considerable intervals; but even a few are proof of a superabundant vitality in a man whose days were usually filled with strenuous mental activity.

Humour and merry-making were often rough on the occasion of a celebration day, as we can gather from an unrestrained scene which Pepys described. Fireworks were thrown with the object of burning fellow guests or neighbours; that done, they blackened each others faces with candlegrease and soot; and, finally, they fell to dancing, the men in women's clothes and vice versa. Small happenings recorded in the Diary enable us to imagine the sportive way in which he treated his familiar companions. Betty Michell, a young married woman, was a special favourite of his. When walking down a street he saw a pretty female figure in front of him going in his direction, and, thinking, wrongly as it turned out, that it was Betty, he gave her a hearty 'clap on the breech'. The incident must have been disconcerting, even to Pepys; and it gives us a valuable insight into the jaunty kind of behaviour that was evidently frequent with him.

9

Valuable Relaxation

———————————⋙⋘———————————

It was, perhaps, natural that Pepys was increasingly successful in striking a satisfactory balance between work and pleasure as he became more proficient at his business, and found that it could be enjoyable. But, at times, he seemed to be unable to distinguish clearly between the kinds of pleasure that are sensible and those that are questionable. In reviewing his behaviour he was inclined to discuss recreation and undue self-indulgence as if there was little distinction in principle between them. It was, no doubt, the strong Puritan streak in him which made him suspect that most pleasures are traps, planned by the Devil.

We may be sure that, without music, Pepys could not have been recognizably the man that he was. The charm of music insinuated itself into his essential being. Nevertheless, he could view it as a threat to his ability to follow his business attentively. There seems to have been no adequate justification for scruples of this kind. His attitude was doubtless a symptom of an oversensitiveness about indulgence in pleasure. One evening, after enjoying a brief interlude of music in a social gathering, following a considerable period in which he had neglected this relaxation, be became 'fearful of being too much taken with musique, for fear of returning to my old dotage thereon, and so neglect my business as I used to do'. Shortly after this he refrained from buying a bass viol 'because of spoiling my present mind and love to business'. Some years later, after enjoying a well-earned evening of recreation, singing songs with the talented actress he so much admired, Mrs. Knepp, his conscience was overactive. 'God forgive me! I do still see that my nature is not to be quite conquered, but will esteem pleasure above all things.'

Once more he was apprehensive of his profession being neglected, when he made a frequently quoted remark: 'However, musique and women I cannot but give way to whatever my business is.' It is significant that dubious relations with women and the beneficial relaxation of music are here assimilated without proper discrimination. In all these instances he displayed a lack of a due sense of proportion. The occasions when music interfered with his professional duties must have been neglible. Another test he applied was rashness in expenditure amounting perhaps to extravagance. If this might occur, then the pleasure must be kept within limits. But, here again, he had no cause to accuse himself, for music did not prove an unduly expensive pastime.

He was, however, usually more sensible; and, during much of the period of the Diary, his singing of songs and playing of musical instruments, alone or with others, constituted an essential part of the pattern of his life, and must have been of immense value in keeping him in good heart. On a number of occasions in 1662 and 1663 he rose very early on spring and summer mornings, and played on his lute or his viol for about an hour before starting work in his office. The effort of getting up at five o'clock in the morning in order to find time for this exercise proves how much in the way of composure it meant to him. A few years later he made a habit of singing a song in the garden, with a musical companion, soon after midday dinner, before returning to the office. This brief 'snap' of music, as he would have called it, must have had a valuable curative effect on him. Asperities and anxieties were thus assuaged or forgotten. Occasionally, on Sundays, and with some regularity in 1664-5, he was enlivened by the visits of two or three musically-minded friends who sang with him in the afternoons or evenings. Psalms, or some songs with a religious flavour, were commonly enjoyed at these times.

Of course, like many people in those days, he frequently delighted

in singing songs, accompanied or unaccompanied, or in playing on a
musical instrument, in the evening, when his day's work was
completed. Sometimes he would feel a special need for playing to
himself in the evening: perhaps he wanted to be calmed and to have
the sense of being comforted. When melancholy, maybe without
knowing why, when 'vexed and cross', when his mind was troubled,
when he was angered at someone's aggravating misbehaviour, or
when he was just worried in a general way by business matters, he
resorted to his lute, violin, viol, or even his flageolet. The last-
mentioned was his solace at the time when the Dutch fleet had
forced its way up the river towards London, and when prospects
were, to say the least, bleak. Even his post at the Navy Board was
endangered. His wife was away in the country, to hide his precious
gold; and, on two evenings or more, he trusted to the effects of his
own soothing music to ease and refresh him.

Several times, when his wife went away for a sojourn at
Brampton, he relied on the strains of a musical instrument to subdue
his sadness. He wrote, on one occasion: 'I up to my wife's closett
and there played upon my viallin a good while . . . sad for want
of my wife whom I love with all my heart, though of late she has
given me some troubled thoughts.' Or his disquiet might be due to
suspicion that all was not well with his absent wife, he having heard
that quarrels were creating dangerous discontents at Brampton;
and a letter from his wife seemed cold. Music was the most salutary
means of relief from such anxieties.

He did not, however, take a narrow view of music. He loved it
for its own sake; and he loved it so much that he wanted to express
himself by singing, by composing songs, and by playing on
numerous musical instruments. Soon after his appointment to the
Navy Board, he took lessons in singing. A year later he was taught
composition, and spent many hours at his 'musique practice' at a
time when he was working strenuously at his office. As the years
passed he added new instruments to his repertoire. It is typical of
him that he was frequently infected with new enthusiasms. The
list of instruments on which he could play grew to include the lute,
theorbo, flute, violin, viol, lyre-viol, flageolet, recorder, spinet, and

triangle.[1] Having listened with much pleasure to the recorder, he bought one 'which I do intend to learn to play on, the sound of it being, of all sounds in the world, most pleasing to me'. Trilling, or quavering, captivated him, so he told his music-master that he was determined to learn how to acquire this accomplishment. Then he heard, being played in a music-room in Whitehall, a new kind of miniature organ. He must have one, cost what it might.

His performances, instrumental, vocal, and in musical composition were intended to give pleasure; and he enjoyed adulation. He was particularly proud of his composition of a song for solo voice, 'Beauty Retire', which Mrs. Knepp sang 'bravely', and 'makes me proud of myself', 'and a very fine song it seems to be'. During several months he reiterated his sense of gratification, and finally remarked that 'without flattery I think it is a very good song'.

When he, alone, or more often with others, sang or played on the leads of his house or in the garden in the late evenings in summer, the sounds could easily be heard by his adjoining neighbours. He consistently assumed that he was providing them with particular enjoyment; and he may, indeed, have been right. One moonlight night, 'we sang till about twelve at night, with mighty pleasure to ourselves and neighbours, their casements opening . . .' Another time, when he played his lute indoors, 'I took much pleasure to have the neighbours come forth into the yard to hear me'. He was not shy at being overheard by strangers. He and his friends would sing when boating on the river. During a visit to Vauxhall Gardens, 'it beginning to be dark, we to a corner and sang, that everybody got about us to hear us . . .' These examples of his vivacity and *naïveté* can help us to imagine him at leisure. If his wife's companion could sing, or his boy, he would gain immense pleasure by singing with them. He once complained to himself: 'I do lack Mercer or somebody in the house to sing with.' Although he occasionally described singing with his wife as pleasurable, her ability in this respect was so slight that it could not give him sustained satisfaction.

He was easily enraptured by fine performances of music. Mrs.

[1] Probably a triangular spinet.

Knepp and others, one evening, bewitched him by their voices. He felt intoxicated, and wished he could 'live and die in it'. 'I spent the night in extasy almost . . .' Again, after listening to the singing of Italian songs by Mrs. Knepp to the accompaniment of the 'harpsicon'—'I do consider that this is all the pleasure I live for in the world, and the greatest I can ever expect in the best of my life . . .' On a visit to the theatre, he found 'mighty pleasant' in a general way a performance entitled *The Virgin Martyr* by Massinger and Dekker. 'But that which did please me beyond any thing in the whole world was the wind-musique when the angel comes down, which is so sweet that it ravished me, and, indeed, in a word, did wrap up my soul so that it made me really sick, just as I have formerly been when in love with my wife; that neither then, nor all the evening going home, and at home I was able to think of any thing, but remained all night transported, so as I could not believe that ever any musick hath that real command over the soul of man as this did upon me: and makes me resolve to practice wind-musique, and make my wife do the like.'

These remarks are most expressive of Pepys's intense disposition. The concluding phrases are, however, a little puzzling, because Pepys had been playing on the flageolet, off and on, for several years; and, in the preceding year, his wife had been taking lessons on the flageolet, and had been playing on this instrument for about six months. He evidently meant to encourage his wife to continue her practice. But this may be one of those quick enthusiasms that gripped him for a brief moment, but which never took practical shape, though the purchase of a recorder, mentioned above, was made shortly after going to *The Virgin Martyr*. We do not know how much he used it.[2]

Listening to the music in *The Virgin Martyr* may well have prompted him to a study of the theory of music in general, for, very soon after his visit to that play, he made an ambitious plan. The self-assurance with which he prepared to attack this problem is typical of one aspect of his character. He mentioned his intention of 'inventing a better theory of musique than hath yet been abroad;

[2] A recorder is much the same kind of instrument as a flageolet.

and I think verily I shall do it'. It was to be a theory 'not yet ever made in the world'. He considered that the existing method by which it was attempted to make music understood was 'ridiculous and troublesome' . . . 'and I know I shall be able hereafter to show the world a simpler way'. He persisted in his endeavours; and the last report we hear of them is in a hopeful strain: 'I am in the right way of unfolding the mystery of this matter, better than ever yet.'

10

A Means of Self-Control

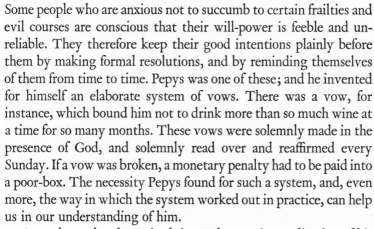

Some people who are anxious not to succumb to certain frailties and evil courses are conscious that their will-power is feeble and unreliable. They therefore keep their good intentions plainly before them by making formal resolutions, and by reminding themselves of them from time to time. Pepys was one of these; and he invented for himself an elaborate system of vows. There was a vow, for instance, which bound him not to drink more than so much wine at a time for so many months. These vows were solemnly made in the presence of God, and solemnly read over and reaffirmed every Sunday. If a vow was broken, a monetary penalty had to be paid into a poor-box. The necessity Pepys found for such a system, and, even more, the way in which the system worked out in practice, can help us in our understanding of him.

As we have already noticed, it was by a strict application of his self-imposed scheme for self-control that he managed to cure himself of a tendency to excessive wine-drinking, which, early in his career, threatened his efficiency by harming his health, and thus diverting his attention unduly from his business. The cure proved to be a permanent one. There was scarcely any return to his old weakness. But the system was not quite so effective when applied to his addiction to playgoing. From time to time there were several, usually shortish, periods of relapse.

At the end of 1661, at the same time that he tackled his

wine-bibbing propensities, he determined to apply a strict limitation to his playgoing. In the summer of 1661 he had described himself as troubled 'that I cannot bring myself to mind my business, but to be too much in love of plays'. It was 'the power of the Devil over me' that drew him to a performance of *The Merry Wives of Windsor*, against, as he alleged, 'my nature and will'. A little later, it was against his 'judgment and conscience' that he went to see a play called *Love and Honour*. Nevertheless he went to see it again twice more in the same week. Many of these performances were in the afternoon; and attendance at them prevented his being present at the office when he might be expected to be there. In the autumn of 1661 he was 'troubled in mind to think how much of late I have addicted myself to expense and pleasure'; and, on the last day of the year, he wrote, in summarizing his situation: 'But my greatest trouble is that I have for this last half year been a very great spend-thrift in all manners of respects.' It was at this stage that he managed to get to grips with himself, and to begin to apply himself strenuously to his work for the Navy.

For the best part of 1662 his vows and his ingrained thriftiness enabled him to keep his playgoing within due limits. Once in the autumn he had to pay a crown into the poor-box, 'and so no harm as to that is done, but only business lost and money lost, and my old habit of pleasure wakened, which I will keep down hereafter, for I thank God these pleasures are not sweet to me now in the very enjoying of them'. Christmas festivities were, however, a little unsettling; and, in early January, he wrote: 'I do find my mind so apt to run its old want of pleasures that it is high time to betake myself to my late vows, which I will tomorrow . . .' But, in the main, his plan succeeded. After an extended period of trial, he said that 'it is a great content to me to see how I am a changed man in all respects for the better' since starting the system.

Various happenings, such as plague, fire, and war, limited the opportunities for playgoing during 1663–6. Moreover, his time was fully occupied by his official business during those years. But by 1667 he required some relief from the strain that he had been under-going. The menace of the Dutch had retreated; and lack of money prevented much enterprise in naval policy. It may well have seemed to him to be a time when a course of pleasure was a good prescription, provided that some sense of discretion was maintained. In April he deemed it prudent to limit the number of his visits to the play, 'I having now seen a play every day this week till I have neglected my business'. During a week in the summer he indulged himself to the same extent; and, in the following week, almost as much. Towards the end of the year he decided that strong measures must be taken, and he began once more 'to bind myself to keep my old vows, and, among the rest, not to see a play till Christmas but once in every other week, and have laid aside £10, which is to be lost to the poor if I do. This I hope in God will bind me, for I find myself mightily wronged in my reputation, and indeed in my purse and business, by my late following of my pleasure for so long a time as I have done.'

It does not require much reading in the Diary to come to the conclusion that Pepys was fond of money. The thought of paying penalties for breach of his vows was, therefore, painful; and it acted as an effective curb, at any rate when the penalty amounted to so considerable a sum as £10. Often he did not try to avoid the issue, and put the money in the pewter box he had specially purchased for the purpose. But at other times he used every possible argument, occasionally of the most specious kinds, to escape an admission that he had broken his oath. This type of prevarication was used almost exclusively in regard to playgoing; and his display of sophistry was apt to be so elaborate as to be ludicrous. He could even go so far as to admit that a particular visit to the play was contrary to the letter of his vow, but allege that it agreed with its sense. After an intricate justification he would come to the conclusion that he was 'not in the least apprehensive that I have done any violence to my oaths'.

A visit to a playhouse that was not in existence when the vow was made raised a nice point in his mind. He sensibly decided that he must pay his forfeit. At first it seemed to him that if he was at a play as the guest of a friend he did not infringe the rules. But it soon became obvious that he would have to make returns for such kindnesses; and as saving of expense was a main object of the scheme, this subterfuge could not be sustained. He was able, however, on one occasion to elude this difficulty, when two Scottish lords took him to a play. As he did not know which of the two paid, and as he had no intention of returning the compliment, his conscience was at ease, and no money had to be put into the pewter box. The height of such sophistical proficiency was reached when he devised the plan of lending a friend the price of tickets for his wife and himself. But, on consideration, he resolved not to be so foolish as to try and deceive himself into adopting this specious evasion. It was, he said, 'a fallacy that I have found now once, to avoyde my vowe with but never to be more practised I swear . . .'

It was sometimes the same with drinking wine. He drank a cup of strong waters 'out of pure conscience to my health', and, for that reason, assumed that his oath did not apply. He also drank burnt wine and even hippocras (sweetened and spiced wine), because these did not come within the category of 'wine'. Hippocras, he said, was 'only a mixed compound drink'.

These elaborate mental gymnastics prove him to have been a considerable master of the art of casuistry. We may wonder how far the flexibility regarding ethical standards which is noticeable in his private life had a counterpart in other kinds of behaviour.

On the whole, the system of vows worked satisfactorily in regard both to wine and playgoing. Pepys evidently thought so, because he extended its application to a number of kinds of conduct in which he often failed to maintain a desired standard of restraint, and even a standard of accomplishment or positive good behaviour. Waste of money, as he considered expenditure on dubious pleasures to be, often made him remorseful; and he found it necessary to invoke his system in order to check tendencies to extravagance. Soon after he had put an end to skylarking proclivities, in the early days of his professional career, he wrote: 'I set to make some strict rules for my future practice in my expenses, which I did bind myself in the presence of God by oath to observe upon penalty therein set down, and I do not doubt but hereafter to give a good account of my time and to grow rich, for I do find a great deal more of content in these few days that I spend well about my business, than in all the pleasure of a whole week, besides the trouble which I remember I always have after that for the expense of my money.'

One of his first ambitions was to be master of a fortune of £1,000. We thus find his oaths about economy having, more than once, reference to the target at which he aimed. Even after a year of commendable steadiness at his business, he found that he was saving very little money. He accordingly determined 'not to be such a fool' as to indulge in ill-considered disbursements 'till I am more warm in my purse, besides my oath of entering into no such expenses till I am worth £1,000'. He also tried to discipline himself into virtuous habits by promising a forfeit if he lay in bed a quarter of an hour after his first waking. This seems to have been an unnecessary extension of the method, for we may gather that he was usually an exemplary early riser. There is but little evidence that he was a constitutional slugabed.

Personal relations with his wife and his behaviour to other members of the female sex were also controlled by the system. As we shall notice later, Pepys seems, at an early stage of his appointment to the Navy Board, to have neglected the need for providing entertainment for his wife's leisure, while he was at the same time spending a good deal of time amusing himself with friends and acquaintances. He came to realize his remissness, and made a vow not to go to the play in future without her. He also hoped to improve her opportunities of recreation by arranging dancing classes. But the problem could not be solved as easily as he thought. His ridiculous jealousy of Pembleton, the dancing-master, brought about a strained situation between his wife and himself. More than once they had 'high words' on the subject; and he sensibly made a vow 'not to oppose her or say anything to dispraise or correct her therein as long as her month [of tuition] lasts, in pain of 2s. 6d. for every time, which, if God pleases, I will observe, for this roguish business has brought us more disquiet than anything [that] has happened a great while'.

A puzzling and surprising aspect of Pepys's system is the slight extent to which he used it in connexion with the most troublesome of all his addictions, his excessive intimacy with women. It is clear from several remarks of his that he did not regard it as venial. This kind of dissipation, however, had not, for him, the same disadvantages that disquieted him in regard to wine-drinking and playgoing. It was not of necessity either expensive or time-absorbing; and these were two mischiefs that seemed to him most undesirable. Although he had a vein of ruthlessness in regard to the treatment of women on whom he had designs, he was as a rule sensitive to the need for magnanimity when his affair was with a woman of modest manners. It is natural, therefore, to find him regretful of his wild behaviour as he reviewed his seduction of the worthy Mrs. Bagwell. On reaching his office after this deplorable episode, he 'with great content' made a vow 'to laisser aller les femmes for a month, and am with all my heart glad to find myself able to come to so good a resolution'. There is an air of complacence in these phrases which is not characteristic of Pepys in general; but it is undoubtedly to be found on several occasions in regard to his amours.

A few days after having made this vow he was giving consideration to the application of another by which he had bound himself to pay a shilling into the poor-box for every time, after the first, that he kissed a woman not related to him. A 'very pretty' lady was present with him at a dinner-party; and he remembered the penalty which he might incur, 'yet I did adventure upon a couple'. He doubtless felt that the forfeit thus incurred was well worth while. But frolicsome conduct like this had but little relation to his systematic efforts to invigorate his self-control.

In the last stages of the period of the Diary, when he had, though not in a very serious way, compromised his wife's personal attendant, Deb, and precipitated a most painful estrangement with his wife, he tried, for some time unavailingly, to restrain himself from contriving secret meetings with the girl. The situation became so serious that strenuous means of self-control were required; and Pepys only secured some assurance of his good behaviour 'having by private vows last night in prayer to God Almighty cleared my mind for the present of the thoughts of going to Deb at Greenwich, which I did long after'.

The final extension of the application of his system was in respect of positive duties of an essential but minor kind, the performance of which he wished to ensure; such matters, for instance, as the payment of petty debts and the collection of petty credits. During the great plague he decided that he must make a new will; but, as he kept putting it off, he bound himself by oath to complete the task within twenty-four hours. He took similar steps in regard to such trivial matters as the clearing up of some private business, and the writing up of his Diary. During the first few years in which the system was operative it was confined to subjects which had an important bearing on his welfare, where considerable will-power was required. But, later, in using vows so as to control his behaviour in regard to minor obligations, he must have found that the solemnity of the system, which had for a considerable period been effective, had lost some of its force.

II

Fears and Anxieties

———————————◄═══►═══◄———————————

The picture of himself that the diarist provides may easily leave the reader with an exaggerated impression of his timorousness. He gives highly realistic descriptions of his tremulous feelings in a variety of circumstances; and it must be acknowledged that occasionally his behaviour was not that of a brave man. Nevertheless, though he may have been terrified at the first onset of a danger, he generally managed to pull himself together and to behave creditably. In this respect he resembled many other people.

On several occasions in his public life he displayed stoutness of spirit and resolution of a high order; notably so when he had to defend the Navy Board, himself included, against vexatious charges before committees and commissioners. His moral, as opposed to physical, courage was undoubted. Two situations illustrate this in a notable way. In October 1666 he argued before the King and Cabinet to the effect that the Navy was in an inefficient condition, and that little could be done by way of remedy without liberal provision of money. As he must have known, this argument would not be well received by some of those whom he addressed. The first part of it would certainly anger Prince Rupert, who had recently been in charge of the main Fleet. He was prepared to face this influential disapproval in the interest of the Service. And, in March 1668, he made his much-praised speech, in front of a possibly hostile House of Commons, in defence of the Navy Board, respecting their alleged maladministration. His speech was a masterpiece of hardihood.

We know, from the Diary, that prior to such formidable experiences he was apt to be faint-hearted in private. When, however, it came to the encounter his courage suddenly blossomed forth. Sometimes, especially later in his career, his ardour not only sustained him in vindicating the Board, but enabled him to show independence and a defiant attitude.

It might be supposed that a man like Pepys, who could, momentarily at least, quail and quiver at a risk to his personal safety, would be lacking in such positive qualities as those of a dynamic administrator, full of plans for efficiency and constructive reform. But, in fact, he displayed these qualities over a considerable period. After he came to be Secretary of the Admiralty his firmness and resolution were notable when he risked incurring the ill will of those undisciplined captains who suffered from the application of his reforming zeal. Naturally, this undaunted rigorousness helped to bring him serious trouble from those who were anxious for his fall.

A sudden, purely physical danger was not one that he was equipped to face with imperturbability. We must remember that he was only a little man; and it would be unreasonable to expect him to face a supposed burglar with the pluck of a prize-fighter. He was not trained, nor was he experienced, in the use of the sword or of fire-arms. The prospect of being embroiled in any sort of battle very naturally frightened him a good deal. On being told, not long after taking possession of his official quarters, that hostile 'Fanatiques' were in the vicinity, he found his neighbours standing armed at their doors. He therefore fetched his sword and pistol, 'though with no good courage at all, but that I might seem not to be afeard'. He had no powder with which to charge his pistol, which was perhaps as well; and, in any case, he was not called upon to defend himself or anyone else. Another time, when large gangs of armed and discontented seamen were said to be in his neighbourhood, he went home 'in great fear', 'expecting to find a tumult about my house, and was doubtful about my riches there'. But all was safe. A little later he heard that seamen were in a mutiny, which put him 'into a great fright'; but here, as in other alarms, he was more concerned for his store of money and his property than for his own person.

After a heated discussion with a choleric and portentous naval commander, Captain (or Major) Holmes, about an appointment to an important post, Holmes hinted at a challenge to a duel; and, as already remarked, Pepys was completely lacking in any training for such adventures. The next day he hopefully described himself as 'merry enough', but the natural fear of such an encounter stuck in his mind. The following day he was 'fearful almost, so poor a spirit I have, of meeting Major Holmes'. There was not much to be ashamed of in these misgivings; and he need not have harboured them, for when they next met Holmes was as anxious as Pepys to be good friends again.

He never pretended that he would enjoy being engaged in warfare. When the Dutch fleet forced its way up the Medway in 1667 his colleagues on the Navy Board were sent there to organize the defences, and he was left in charge of the office. He was frankly relieved to be so situated, 'near my own house and out of danger, yet in a place of doing the King good service'. As he came to middle age, however, he must have grown out of such misgivings. During his stay at Tangier in 1683, although in no way required to do so, he did not hesitate to inspect the dispositions of the Moors, and to run some risk of being shot at or taken prisoner.

Few circumstances can be more intimidating than those of being set on by a large dog. When he was on foot going to Greenwich he was so attacked; and the animal seemed to be taking a fancy to his legs, as it got hold of his garters. Looking back on the incident, he considered that he should have kept his head better and remembered his sword. But happily he did not.

Both the Plague of 1665 and the Great Fire of 1666 gave plenty of opportunities to timid people to show cowardice. Pepys emerged from both these crises with a considerable amount of credit. During the Plague he stayed at his post in Seething Lane when many other officials had moved into the suburbs, or farther afield; and he was proud of his steadfastness. This did not imply that he was not afraid. The situation was calculated to frighten any normal person. He made such remarks as 'the plague growing very raging and my apprehensions of it great'. Two or three times he was thoroughly alarmed in case he had been in contact with infected people. When a boy was thought to be sick of the plague in a house in which he was staying he wondered whether he could make his escape to some other lodging. 'However I thought it not fit for me to discover too much fear to go away, nor had I any place to go to.' When the plague was subsiding he nearly entered an infected house in Chelsea by accident. 'So we with great affright turned back . . .; and went away (I for my part in great disorder) for Kensington . . .'

In the Great Fire he seems to have shown no more signs of alarm than his neighbours. Perhaps he showed less, because he was able to keep his head enough, not only to advise the King about safety measures, but to make careful and sensible arrangements for the securing of his own movable property. He was, however, as many circumstances indicate, of a highly nervous temperament. The Great Fire left its mark on him for a long time. Several months after he was kept awake at night by 'great terrors of fire'; once 'till almost two in the morning', and, another time, 'mightily troubled the most of the night with fears of fire'.

The fondness that Pepys had for money becomes evident in a variety of situations. Perhaps his fear of outrage and violence was most intense when his stored gold in his dwelling-house seemed to be in danger. For several years in succession he was frightened from time to time by strange nocturnal noises which seemed to him to be likely to be those of robbers in the process of searching for his cherished riches. The first time the suspicious sounds were eventually found to proceed from the activities of an inquisitive dog. Next, they proved to be those of the maids going to bed at an inordinately late hour. An equally unexpected explanation was the sweeping of a neighbour's chimney in the dead of night. He would, he said, have gone to investigate the strange creaking at the outset, 'but my wife would not let me. Besides, I could not do it without making a noise . . .'

His house, he realized, was very vulnerable to burglars. There were many possible ways of entry, including windows reached by way of the leads. His wife warned him that, for several nights, she had heard unaccountable noises, and sent for him to come home from the office one evening, where he had been working late. 'So at almost two o'clock, I home to my house, and in great fear to bed, thinking every running of a mouse really a thiefe; and so to sleep, very brokenly, all night long, and found all safe in the morning.' Apprehensions of this kind must have afflicted many well-off people in and around the City of London in those days, for there would have been a good many who, for some sensible reason, had to keep much of their money in coin, secreted in their dwelling-houses.

There were also circumstances which would induce in him a state of trepidation, although there was no apparent risk of physical harm. When threatened with arrest in a matter in which he had no personal responsibility, he was penetrated with fright on being suddenly confronted in the street with a potentially disagreeable person, and found himself starting with agitation 'at hearing one man cough behind my neck'. Ghost stories before going to bed had such an untoward effect on him when he was spending the night with colleagues at a dockyard that he was 'almost afeard to lie alone'. It is at least possible that his liking for vivid description of this kind of incident may mislead us into overestimating the extent of his perturbation.

The terrors that Pepys experienced in his private affairs were usually of brief duration. But, in national affairs, anxiety for the future often predominated over immediate dangers. When there was cause for such anxiety he was inclined to be deeply dejected, though not perhaps more so than some of his colleagues. Such a situation prevailed in 1666, when the lack of funds for keeping the Navy in an efficient state imperilled the nation's safety. 'This is', he said, 'every day a greater and greater omen of ruine. God fit us for it . . . the end thereof must be speedy ruine.' And he concluded that he would be well content to retreat to his family home at Brampton, and spend the rest of his life there in modest, but, he hoped, safe retirement. A few days later he thought that he could foresee 'great unhappiness coming upon us'. Early in the next year he deplored the decision 'to keep but a flying fleete this year [for lack of funds]; which, it may be may preserve us a year longer, but the end of it must be ruin'. When, in the summer of 1667, the Dutch had broken through our defences in the Medway, and burnt some of our ships, the peril was more pressing, and he wrote: 'And the truth is, I do fear so much that the whole kingdom is undone, that I do this night resolve to study with my father and wife what to do with the little that I have in money by me . . . So God help us! and God knows what disorders we may fall into, and whether any violence on this office, or perhaps some severity on our persons . . .' This sounds defeatist; but it must be remembered that Pepys might reasonably have expected, according to the available information, that the Dutch forces would break through to London. They certainly had a fair opportunity to do so, for our military forces were inadequate, and national morale low. Pepys's attitude was shared by a number of intelligent people.

His liability to dejection is clearly attributable to a highly sensitive nature. This, with its tendency to excitability, had the unfortunate effect of making him anxious about relatively inconsiderable matters which did not merit expenditure of nervous energy. He was, in fact, capable of being a great worrier, as the following entry proves: 'Lay long in bed discoursing with my wife about her mayds, which by Jane's going away in discontent and against my opinion do make some trouble between my wife and me. But these are but foolish troubles and so not to be set to heart, yet it do disturb me mightily these things.'

The amenities of his official residence, although a subject of minor importance, bulked largely in his mind, and caused him a great deal of unnecessary distress. As a result of some rearrangements in the quarters of the Commissioners, Pepys was in risk of losing some advantages, and even some accommodation. The possible deprivation of his use of the leads (flat roof) put him into 'so great a disquiet' that he lost a whole night's sleep. And, when the threat was repeated later, he lost another night's sleep. Even trivial problems had the same effect. He was asked to be a godfather

to a child of Sir W. Batten's sister. He felt that he did not want to
undertake this, probably because of the expense, but could not well
refuse. 'Which, however, did trouble me very much to be at charge
to no purpose, so that I could not sleep hardly all night, but in the
morning I bethought myself, and I think it is very well I should do it.'

He might have learnt from experience, but he did not. Sometimes
it looks as if he was searching for something to worry about. At the
end of a long entry recording a day's activities, he wrote: 'and so to
supper and to bed vexed at two or three things, viz.: That my
wife's watch proves so bad as it do; the ill state of the office; and
Kingdom's business [? in regard to naval prizes]; at the charge
which my mother's death for mourning will bring me when all paid.'
He could admit to himself how stupid he was being; but this did
not seem to help him to control himself and be more sensible.

There were times when he had real grounds for anxiety, especially when public inquiries were being made into the administrative irregularities of the Navy Board, including such embarrassing
matters as profit-making and acceptance of bribes by Navy Commissioners. He felt that he was peculiarly unfitted to face anxieties
such as these. 'I do find so poor a spirit within me', he remarked,
'that it makes me almost out of my wits, and puts me to so much
pain, that I cannot think of anything, nor do anything but vex and
fret, and imagine myself undone, so that I am ashamed of myself to
myself, and do fear what would become of me if any real affliction
should come upon me.' Another time: 'I do plainly see my weakness that I am not a man able to go through trouble, as other men,
but that I should be a miserable man if I should meet with adversity,
which God keep me from!'

Reflections of this kind hardly seem to be those of a man capable
of calm detachment in a serious emergency. And yet Pepys, on
several occasions of national peril, showed that he could read an
abstruse book, experiment with a scientific apparatus, or play on a
musical instrument, when many people in his situation could not
have quietened their minds sufficiently to do these things. These
were occasions of public crisis; and doubtless he considered that,
when he had done all that he could in his particular sphere, he had

best relax. At the time when the dangers of the Dutch continuing their course up the River Medway in 1667 were at their most pressing, he had spent the day at the dockyards trying to organize the provision of fire-ships. On returning home, 'as long as it was light, reading Mr. Boyle's book of Hydrostatics, which is a most excellent book as ever I read . . . When it grew too dark to read I lay down and took a nap . . . and after having wrote to Sir W. Coventry an account of what I had done and seen . . . I to bed.' Twice, within the next day or two, he eased the strain by playing on his flageolet at home.

We frequently find that when he was actually involved in serious trouble his behaviour was exemplary. His expectation that he would not be able to meet personal affliction and adversity with a brave face was proved to be false, for in his later career he suffered imprisonment and loss of office with remarkable fortitude and dignity.

During his earlier professional life, as well as later on, Pepys suffered a good deal from ill health; and this may have tended to make him hypersensitive, especially in his relations with his colleagues. He was highly susceptible to chills, often with the result that he suffered extreme and protracted constipation, and also irregularity in passing water. These were plights which might easily have produced a state of wretchedness even in stout-hearted persons. He did not minimize the pain and inconvenience he experienced. But he did not pose as a martyr. On the few occasions when he was prevented by such illness from attending to his work he made bold efforts to return to it with the least possible delay. In his second Diary, too, we get an impression of his courage during some unpleasant spells of indisposition at Tangier.

On many occasions he attributed particular reasons for his catching cold. He evidently thought it important to trace the cause, so as to avoid a repetition. His careful inferences do not necessarily imply fussiness, but they certainly indicate that his susceptibility was extreme. Incidentally, his descriptions of the circumstances in which these ailments were contracted reflect his manner of life in some minor respects; and, in spite of our sympathy for him, it is impossible to avoid smiling at the oddness of the causes of some of his transient maladies.

He suffered much pain, 'having a great fit of the colic', as a result, he thought, of 'having catched cold yesterday by putting off my stockings to wipe my toes'. A few months later, he had forgotten this lesson; and he considered a cause of his illness had been 'sitting too long bare-legged to pare my corns'. Even the briefest exposure of his legs to the air seemed fraught with risk, for he 'most certainly' caught a cold 'by my staying a little too long bare-legged yesterday morning when I rose while I looked out fresh socks and thread stockings'.

Contact of his feet with water could also be perilous. He was in a rash mood when, returning from Deptford in a small boat on a warm June day, he dangled his legs in the river. The result was not merely a cold, but internal troubles and 'great pain'. More than once the mere washing of his feet at home caused cold and griping. Naturally enough, the removal of his periwig without taking due precautions was likely to produce a pain in the head. This could also happen when someone was washing his ears, or as a result of 'flinging off my hat at dinner, and sitting with the wind in my neck'.

These detailed records of personal mischances are perhaps chiefly valuable in illustrating his meticulous way of studying his health and the means of avoiding illness. But when we read that he feared that he had taken cold in walking in a damp room while 'it is in washing', we may well wonder whether his inclination to be a worrier did not extend to health as well as to domestic problems, business, and politics.

He maintained an ardent interest in the diagnosis of the symptoms of physical defects and ailments, based on analyses of his experiences. This is well illustrated in his notes on 'The Present State of My Health', written in 1677, and preserved among the Rawlinson MSS. We must not forget that, as a Fellow of the Royal Society, he had a reputation for interest in scientific research; and he was always ready to encourage and, as far as he had opportunities, to pursue studies in that direction. His most obvious field for inquiry was his own physical condition.

12

Decorum and the Lack of It

In Pepys's opinion licentious behaviour was unpardonable and even disgraceful, if, through lack of discretion, it became a matter of public knowledge. But the same behaviour kept secret was a different affair altogether. The person so conducting himself might subsequently have reason to regret what he had done, but as there would be nothing notorious about it, the action was not reprehensible. Pepys was not a Tartuffe; but they had a certain similarity, for Tartuffe remarked: 'The public scandal is what constitutes the offence: sins sinned in secret are no sins at all.'

Lord Sandwich's liaison with Betty Becke at Chelsea shocked Pepys because it was carried on in so public a way, and thus became capable of harming his reputation. The terms in which he expressed disgust at this conduct can easily dispose readers to smile or raise their eyebrows in view of their knowledge of his own extensive improprieties. Pepys spoke of 'the whole business of my Lord's folly with this Mrs. Becke at Chelsea, of all which I am ashamed to see my Lord so grossly play the beast and fool', and of his having 'his private lust undisturbed with this common whore'—a description for which there seems to be little or no justification.

Similarly, he was deeply shocked by the reports of Charles II's unrestrained conduct, which was a matter of some notoriety, and freely discussed by people at Court, and even outside it. When he heard that the King was seen clambering over the wall of Somerset

House by night, presumably to visit the Duchess of Richmond, he described this as 'a horrid shame'. The shame was in the publicity. He himself sometimes indulged in similar activities in not very creditable circumstances, and in less imposing surroundings. But his liaisons with women caused him no more than transient twinges of conscience, because no one knew anything about them.

Any coarseness in public behaviour or general conversation offended him. He was distressed to see a young clergyman sitting down to dinner having previously drunk so much as to be inebriated. A new play aroused his dislike, 'it being very smutty'. But he enjoyed reading in secret a highly improper French book, although he pretended that he regarded it merely with a curious eye. It was 'the most bawdy, lewd book that ever I saw'. At first, he was ashamed to do more than dip into it. Later, he read it through, and decided that it was 'not amiss for a sober man once to read over to inform himself in the villainy of the world'. Finally, he burnt it so that there should be no traces left of this dubious exploit in sociological research.

Feminine modesty attracted him in various ways. If an engaging young woman proved sportive and playful, but at the same time made it clear that she would not allow him to take undue liberties, he expressed himself as pleased; and he respected and admired her all the more. But if, by insinuation and blandishment, he could gradually break down the defences of modesty, his pleasure was even greater. He found the project of inveigling a demure young woman to be entrancing. On the other hand, he gained no satisfaction in an easy victory. Shamelessness disenchanted him, for he at once suspected a courtesan. When Betty Lane, though allowing him some liberties, kept him in check, he said that 'I much commend and like her'; but when she was more free with him he regarded her as dissolute and lacking in proper reserve. And, later, when she sought him out and was prepared to abandon herself to him, he grew frightened and determined to keep away from her for some time. If there was any conquering to be done, he was to be the conqueror. He won his way at his own pleasure, in his own time, and with due regard to prudence.

It was a different story with Mrs. Bagwell, the worthy and respectable wife of a naval carpenter. She was constantly importuning Pepys to obtain a better appointment for her husband; and this gave him an advantage which he did not overlook. At first he acted with restraint, 'she being, I believe, a very modest woman'. Later, he made some advances, but 'very modestly she denied me, which I was glad to see and shall value her the better for it, and I hope never to tempt her to any evil more'. But, within three months, by relentless pressure, and by availing himself of her concern for her husband's promotion, he had seduced her.

Men of Pepys's social standing, or a better, sometimes took it upon them to fondle young women who were a little lower in the social scale without there being any cause for reflection on the latter's modesty. Pepys was much attached to Betty Michell, a young married friend, and often embraced her. In terms that may seem a little strange today, he remarked: 'I find her mighty modest. But I had her lips as much as I would . . .' After a dinner at which two captivating young women were present, there was 'merry kissing and looking on their breasts, and all the innocent pleasure in the world'. His beloved Deb, at one of their last meetings, allowed him some tender caresses, 'but she mighty coy, and I hope modest'. Terminology in regard to such episodes varies from age to age.

The lustfulness that Pepys so frequently displayed amounted to an abnormality; and it is natural to seek for some explanation of it. This peculiarity is all the more curious because he was a man of fine sensibilities and a cultivated mind. It seems almost impossible that such a person could indulge in the sordid intrigues which he seemed quite unable to resist. An eminent medical authority has suggested that his lecherous propensities have a physiological explanation connected with the operation he underwent for stone when in his twenty-sixth year. It may well be, therefore, that there is a good deal of ground for extenuating his conduct.

In the earlier stages in the history of his amorous adventures he felt some pricks of conscience; and, on at least three occasions, after taking considerable liberties with Betty Lane, he expressed to himself his sense of shame and his intention never to do the same again. But with an increasing number of adventures behind him he ceased, it seems, to be troubled with disquieting thoughts. In the circumstances there seems to be little object in trying to discuss the moral aspect. It is enough here to notice briefly the amazing ardour, and even indefatigability, he displayed.

On a winter's day in 1665 he spent a busy morning which included his attendance on the Duke of York in Whitehall, where he and other members of the Navy Board gave the Duke such information as he required, and answered questions. Then, at his barber's, he made an assignation with 'my Jane' for the next Sunday. Jane suggested the rendezvous, 'but to see how modestly and harmlessly she brought it out was very pretty'. Next, at a tavern, he sported with the young kinswoman of the proprietress 'without hurt'. From there to Betty Lane (now Betty Martin, and married) where 'I did *ce que je voudrais avec* her most freely, and it having cost 2*s.* in wine and cake upon her, I away sick of her impudence . . .' Thence he went to a dinner-party at Lord Brouncker's, at which he was evidently the life and soul of the party, occasioning much mirth with a ballad he brought with him.

He was adept at intermixing his amours with his business, or with other pleasures; and he had a remarkable ability for transferring his energy and emotion rapidly from one to the other. Only a few days after the Great Fire, at a time when his professional affairs were not pressing, but when the reorganization of his household had been occupying much of his attention, he could indulge in two amours a day. In the morning '*tout ce que je voudrais*' with Betty Martin again; and the same in the afternoon with Mrs. Bagwell. He was, indeed, exuberant and tireless.

There were situations, it would seem, when he could enjoy regarding feminine beauty with detachment, perhaps moved mainly by aesthetic considerations. One of his favourite diversions can be described as 'gazing on women'. It is only fair to assume that he then had no ulterior motives, because his gazing was practised chiefly during services in church on Sundays. On two occasions he went to Clerkenwell Church to gaze on *La belle Boteler*, as the famous beauty, Frances Butler, was sometimes styled. He managed the second time to sit in the next pew, and regarded her as 'one I do very much admire myself for my choice of her as a beauty, she having the best lower part of her face that ever I saw all the days of my life'. On a round of churches, he visited the French Church, 'where much pleased with the three sisters of the parson, very handsome, especially in their noses, and sing prettily'. He was, we may suppose, something of a connoisseur.

He would spend all the sermon-time and much of the rest of the service in gazing on his chosen beauty, if it were only 'the fine milliner's wife'. Once or twice he went a little further than gazing, but only to hold a hand, or follow the lady home to see where she lived. He evidently had no regard for what might be thought of him as a starer, for he wrote on one occasion: 'I did entertain myself with my perspective glass up and down the church by which I had the great pleasure of seeing and gazing at a great many very fine women; and what with that and sleeping, I passed away the time till sermon was done . . .'

There were other opportunities in which he could practise the pastime of gazing. He sat close to Mrs. Palmer (later Lady Castlemaine), the King's mistress, at a dull and badly acted play, 'and filled my eyes with her, which much pleased me'. And, on the royal occasion of the Queen's coming to town by river from Hampton Court, 'that which pleased me best was, that my Lady Castlemaine stood over against us upon a piece of White Hall, where I glutted myself with looking on her'. His interest in feminine beauty was, it seems, partly speculative, for he could enjoy gazing wistfully, and for a considerable time, on an artist's representation of a bewitching face. When his wife's portrait was being painted in a studio 'I the while stood looking on a pretty lady's picture, whose face did please me extremely'.

We may feel sure that his interest in feminine beauty was often based exclusively on principles of art. Something amounting to mixed feelings of anger and disgust affected him when he saw women in whom he was interested, or whom he admired, with their faces painted. For a long time he was friendly with Mrs. Pierce, the wife of an old friend, and sometime Surgeon-General of the Fleet.

He had, with many others, thought her extremely pretty. But when she started 'making up' he became violently incensed. He could 'loathe her' and 'hate her, that I thank God I take no pleasure in her at all more'. Even when he saw two actresses with painted faces on visiting the back of the stage he was equally excited. 'But Lord! to see how they were both painted would make a man mad, and did make me loathe them.' It may be that it was the impairment of female beauty by some artificial means that exasperated him in so extraordinary a manner. He was angry when his wife insisted on wearing artificial, light-coloured locks of hair, and eventually persuaded her to give them up. There is a possibility that painted lips and cheeks might have amounted to an impediment to kissing; and he was as ardent and enterprising a kisser as he was a gazer.[1]

[1] Pepys, with his puritanical attitude, would dislike such an innovation as painting of faces on principle. John Evelyn wrote in his diary (11 May 1654): 'I now observed how the women began to paint themselves, formerly a most ignominious thing and used only by prostitutes.'

13

Kindness Preponderant

———————⟢⟣———————

Perhaps the most critical test of anyone's character is a comparison of the exercise of his kindness with any addiction on his part to harshness or malice. Pepys emerges safely from this scrutiny, though, as is natural, he cannot escape some charges of inconsiderateness; and these are specially pertinent in regard to his wife. His relations with her will be noticed separately in later chapters. Meanwhile, we may quote some instances of his kindness and lack of kindness in other respects.

With his excitable temperament, he naturally acted at times both precipitately and in an ill-considered fashion. The instances given in the Diary are few; and it is not likely, owing to his complete frankness, that anything remarkable of this kind has been omitted. Apart from incidents affecting his wife, his loss of temper seems chiefly to have been confined to his treatment of his domestic servants. It is notable that, in his professional activities, he nearly always recognized the importance of only acting with due deliberation. Stupidity and inefficiency in his maid-servants sometimes induced outbreaks of temper, for which he was soon sorry. Usually his relations with them were excellent; and it is a pity that, now and then, he allowed himself to lose control with people who had no means of redress other than giving notice to leave, which might not be convenient to them. But they evidently realized that these outbreaks had no serious significance, and that he had human frailties like most people.

He could be suddenly enraged at so small a matter as the unsatisfactory way in which a maid did her house-work. 'I took a broom and basted her till she cried extremely, which made me vexed, but before I went out I left her appeased.' When there had been some mistake about the proper time for getting up in the morning he was uncontrolled enough to declare that he could kick a maid downstairs, a threat that she 'mumbled at mightily'. In dressing himself one morning, he discovered that all his bands were so 'ill-smoothed' that 'I crumpled them and flung them on the ground, and was angry with Jane, which made the poor girl mighty sad, so that I was troubled for it afterwards'.

None of these incidents caused any great harm, or disclosed any vicious traits. Quick temper was shown, and was soon followed by proper regret. There were, however, two instances where he appeared in a more unfavourable light. The mere fact that an objectionable Scottish woman was let into the house to help the maids prompted him to have 'our little girle' beaten, 'and then we shut her down into the cellar, and there she lay all night'. Some time later Luce, the cook-maid, had left the front door and hatch open 'which so vexed me that I did give her a kick in our entry and offered a blow at her'. He did not appear to be sorry for this lamentable conduct, but was only vexed that it had been seen by his neighbour's footboy, who might tell his employers about it. Pepys's description of his attempt to gloss over the incident is typical of his ability to act a part. He 'did put on presently a very pleasant face to the boy, and spoke kindly to him, as one without passion, so as it may be he might not think I was angry . . .' In considering the significance of this and similar conduct, we should, no doubt, bear in mind that it was the custom in those days to chastise refractory domestics.

He had for some years a boy-servant, Will Wayneman. He sometimes found good reason to belabour the boy with vigour, for he was a mischievous young rascal. But, on the whole, Pepys's treatment of him was distinguished by extraordinary patience and forbearance. Time and again the boy deserved to be dismissed, but be was repeatedly forgiven and allowed another chance to reform.

It is obvious, from many passages in the Diary, that Pepys's maid-servants were generally devoted to him; and he was almost uniformly attached to them; sometimes, indeed, unduly affectionate with them. His genuine kindliness for them frequently became conspicuous when they were leaving his service—often because of his wife's disapproval of their behaviour. When this happened he made some such remark as 'I could hardly forbear weeping to think of her going'. 'The wench cried, and I was ready to cry too . . .' His wife's women companions were generally cultured; and he treated them as friends. Parting with them was an even more personal matter. Especially was this so when the sociable and musical Mary Mercer left. 'I after dinner went up to my chamber and there could have cried to myself, had not people come to me about business.' He was as much distressed for Deb as for himself when his wife discovered him embracing and kissing her. The account of this episode in the Diary includes such phrases as 'my mind mighty troubled for the poor girle, whom I fear I have undone by this'; 'I have reason to be sorry and ashamed of it, and more to be troubled for the poor girl's sake, whom I fear I shall by this means prove the ruin of, though I shall think myself concerned both to love and be a friend to her'; 'I shall love and pity her'; 'she is indeed my sacrifice, poore girle'.

He spoke once of his regret at losing even an unsatisfactory maid, 'partly through my love to my servants'; and this claim is certainly sustainable. When his boy, Tom, who had grown up in his service, was to marry his maid, Jane, he told them that he would give Tom £40 and Jane £20, and that his wife would give Jane £20 more, to set them up in married life. This was generous treatment.

If we were able to know the opinions of the maids in Pepys's employment regarding their master, we should undoubtedly have an enhanced view of him. His qualities of unassuming friendliness, of cheerfulness breaking into jollity, and his natural sympathy must have endeared him to his household. Even if the thought of doing so occurred to him, he could hardly feel like enlarging on these

qualities in the Diary; but they are obvious to the sensitive reader.
A biography by a contemporary might have enlightened us in this
respect; but, alas! there is none. The later history of his life confirms
his ability to evoke the affection and loyalty of his servants. A
notable instance of this is to be found in a letter from an old servant,
Mary Ballard, who, on hearing, shortly before his death, that
he was seriously ill, offered to come back into his service so as to
help nurse him, although she was married and had a home of her
own.

In general, Pepys's relations with his clerks at the office, as with
his domestics, were extremely happy. He treated them in friendly
fashion; and, after a few years in his post, he made a habit of having
some of them to dinner in his house from time to time. By that
means 'I have opportunity to talk with them about business, and I
love their company very well'. They often had good discourse
together and were merry. He also found these to be useful occasions
for obtaining technical information; and he sometimes obtained
valuable advice from them about proposed official action, or the
form of a memorandum or a letter.

He would take trouble to assist them in their private affairs.
Thomas Hater (or Hayter), one of his senior clerks, had several
reasons to be grateful to him. He arranged for his appointment to
better posts than those which he had been holding. When Hater
was in a considerable predicament, having been detected at a
meeting of Friends, against the law, he helped him with advice and
secured for him the invaluable protection of the Duke of York.
Hater thanked Pepys 'for all the love and kindness I have shewed
him hitherto', at which Pepys was deeply moved. Their association
was particularly pleasant and intimate. Pepys relied on Hater for
assistance in many perplexing official problems, and often took him
home to dinner. He had complete confidence in him, and put him
in charge of his store of money in his house when circumstances
were hazardous. When Hater's house was burnt down in the Great
Fire, Pepys took him in and put him to bed. Sad to say, Hater, on
being put to the test at a time when Pepys was being harried by his
enemies in the sixteen-seventies, proved to be unreliable and a

time-server. But Pepys, being in a position later on to retaliate, showed praiseworthy restraint.

Another senior clerk in the Navy Office, not under Pepys, but under the Comptroller, was Thomas Turner. They were neighbours, in the block of official residences in Seething Lane, and were constantly in touch with each other, both officially and socially. Turner had expected to obtain the post of Clerk of the Acts when Pepys was brought in from outside; and he evidently nurtured feelings of envy for a long time afterwards. He even attempted some small intrigues for the benefit of himself and to the detriment of Pepys. Sir William Penn supported Turner, and appears to have allied himself with this discontented man in efforts to deprive Pepys of some of the traditional privileges of his post.

In the early contacts between the two men Pepys acted with indulgent forbearance; and, although the office of 'purveyour of petty provisions' was incorporated in his own post of Clerk of the Acts, he allowed Turner to have the purveying, 'because I would not have him lose the place'. He soon learnt, however, that Turner was dissatisfied with his position and was making sly complaints to Sir W. Penn and others. Turner, on his part, considered that Pepys was plotting against him.

Later on Pepys sent for Turner, 'and I told him my whole mind, and how it was in my power to do him a discourtesy about his place of petty purveyance, and at last did make him see (I think) that it was his concernment to be friendly to me and what belongs to me'. Many months after this there was still considerable tension between the two of them. Pepys was outspoken with Turner, and hinted at the effect of Turner's behaviour according as it was favourable or unfavourable to him and his clerks, 'which I doubt not but will operate well'. Animosity continued to smoulder, and even threatened to break out again; and Pepys decided that he must be stern. 'Among other things Mr. Turner making his complaint to me how my clerks do all the worke and get all the profit, and he hath no comfort, nor cannot subsist, I did make him apprehend how he is beholding to me more than to any body for my suffering him to act as Pourveyour of petty provisions, and told him so largely my little value of any body's favour, that I believe he will make no complaints a good while.'

It was not long after this encounter that Turner became seriously apprehensive of the risk of his being put out of his official residence by a member of the Navy Board who required one. Pepys remarked that if this happened it would be hard on the Turners, 'and though I love him not, yet for his family's sake I pity him'. This threat hung over the Turners for many months; and they came to Pepys for advice, instead of going, for instance, to Penn, who had been, so to speak, in league with him. 'I did give them the best advice, poor people, that I could, and would do them any kindnesse, though it is strange that now they should have ne'er a friend of Sir W. Batten or Sir W. Pen to trust but me, that they have disobliged.' Eventually, the Turners were put out of their house, and Pepys managed to arrange that they should have a rent allowance in lieu.

The final phases in the relationship between the two men were not happy. Pepys secured for Turner the remunerative post of Storekeeper at Deptford. The Turners should, he thought, have known whose influence it was that brought them this good fortune; and he considered them to be ungrateful; 'but let it go: if they do not own it, I shall have it in my hand to teach them to do it'. He tried hard to be consistently charitable to the Turners; but he could not sustain the part. There was evidently an inveterate antipathy between them.

Will Hewer was not only Pepys's confidential clerk, he was also his personal assistant, his aide-de-camp, so to speak. The relations between them serve to elucidate the complexity of Pepys's character even more effectively than those with Turner. Will was seventeen years old when first employed by Pepys in 1660. He lived for some three years as an inmate in Pepys's house, and was always at his beck and call. It is plain that he was a young man of character, and of an independent turn of mind. His social status was at least equal to that of Pepys.

Although he certainly became sincerely attached to Pepys from the start, he was not prepared to be subjected to constant petty restraints and controls; in fact, he considered that he was entitled to be treated as an adult with thoughts and feelings of his own. When he was chided for returning home too late in the evening, he was truly sorry to have made his master angry, and he shed tears. This is proof that he was not of a pert or insolent temperament. But he liked to be free to dress and behave as if he had a reasonable measure of independence. Pepys objected once or twice to this kind of freedom, being 'much offended in mind at a proud trick Will hath got, to keep his hat on in the house . . . I fear I shall be troubled by his pride and laziness, though in other things he is good enough'.

Another ground for remonstrance by Pepys was Will's walking with his cloak flung over his shoulder, 'like a Ruffian'. This was no more than a harmless piece of youthful swagger. Pepys told him that this deportment was immodest; and Will replied that it was not. Whereupon Pepys lost his temper and boxed Will's ears twice, 'which I never did before, and so was after a little troubled at it'. But he used the same injudicious method of reproof on other occasions when the supposed offences do not seem to have warranted physical punishment. Will was evidently expected to treat his master, and mistress too, in a submissive and almost obsequious manner; and he was accordingly charged with showing insufficient respect, and also lack of consideration.

In these early years of his employment Will sometimes felt that he must rebel. When told by Mrs. Pepys to attend church in company with the maids, he refused, saying that he would not be made a slave of. And, here, he seems to have prevailed. In some ways, however, he was remarkably pliant. He came home one night and went to bed ill. Pepys suspected that he was intoxicated; and, on this mere suspicion, summoned him from his bed for interrogation, which Will was able to meet satisfactorily. But he made no complaint about this inconsiderate treatment.

Will's position in Pepys's household was most unsatisfactory. He was too continuously under the immediate eye of his master; and he was thrown, very unsuitably, into the company of the maids, in whom he was not much interested. Pepys came to the conclusion that his 'family' was 'mighty out of order by this fellow Will's corrupting the mayds by his idle talk and carriage'. And Will was unhappy because he realized that he was not being appreciated, and was even being considered to be a source of irritation. Pepys decided that it would be better on all hands for Will to live in lodgings, and to attend at the office, having only occasional duties in the house. Will packed his things and received some kind words from his master. Once more he showed his affection and fidelity by shedding tears.

After this change, the situation was much improved; and Will but rarely found cause for any discontent. He was able to enjoy the liberty he wanted. At the same time he increasingly proved himself to be a loyal, faithful, and helpful assistant, a part which he was to sustain for many years. Pepys, on his side, reposed more and more confidence in him, and treated him in all respects as a friend, being constantly invited to dinner or supper, and joining in evenings' entertainment or recreation. When an offer of a good post was made for Pepys to fill from his clerks, he decided not to propose Will, because 'I do believe he will not part with me, nor have I any mind to part with him'.

Will became of considerable use in discussing puzzling aspects of business, and was able to make valuable suggestions to Pepys in regard to the drafting of official memoranda. Though Pepys made some querulous remarks about his secretarial abilities, it is obvious that he appreciated his discerning comments. There was little that he would not undertake where Pepys's interest was involved. He proved invaluable in helping to compose marital difficulties. When Pepys was in sore distress, being tormented by his wife as a result of his being found by her embracing Deb, Will behaved with great discretion and helpfulness, far beyond what might have been expected of him. Only a deep affection for Pepys could have disposed him to act as he did.

No doubt Pepys has painted an unduly unattractive picture of himself in his treatment of Will. He has with meticulous accuracy described his strictures and occasional lack of proper consideration. He has mentioned the aggravations, and his displays of anger. But he does not give any adequate impression of his own undoubted kindliness and warmth of heart. We have only to read between the lines to be assured that these qualities were displayed. It would have been almost impossible for Will to have been so devoted to him if he had been harsh or even cold-hearted.

Pepys evidently set himself to gain a reputation for benevolence in his dealings with poor and distressed naval folk who came to the office seeking relief; and he seems to have succeeded. Not long after his appointment, he wrote: 'It is my content that by several hands today I have the name of good-natured man among the poor people that come to this office.' He tried to be fair in his financial dealings with subordinates. An anchor-smith had paid him 'fifty pieces in gold' to be recommended for promotion. The recommendation was ineffective because the man could not undertake the post offered. Pepys 'in honour and conscience' repaid the money, even though the man protested, 'and I am glad to have given him so much cause to speake well of me'. When the Clerk of the Rope-yard at Woolwich died, his widow entreated the friendship of the Navy Board, 'which we shall, I think in every thing do for her. I am sure I will.' Again, in the case of the sudden death by drowning of Captain Batters, a captain of a fire-ship, he wrote about this sad accident; and, after mentioning several items in his day's activities, his mind reverted to the sad occurrence, and he added a brief and significant sentence: 'Sorry for poor Batters.' This spontaneous outburst is good proof of a genuine sympathy.

When wives of naval prisoners of war in Holland were in dire need, and came to the Navy Office clamouring for help, he was troubled at his inability to relieve them. 'I confess their cries were so sad for money . . . that I do most heartily pity them, and was ready to cry to hear them, but cannot helpe them. However, when the rest were gone, I did call one to me that I heard complaine only and pity her husband and did give her some money, and she blessed me and went away.'

Plenty of evidence, too, can be adduced for his practical sympathy in the distresses of his friends and relations. He took a great deal of trouble to prevent the forfeiture of the estate of a widowed cousin whose husband was thought to have committed suicide. His wife's relations were a frequent cause of anxiety; and he sometimes helped them with money. When her parents were going to live for a time in France, he sent them three Jacobuses in gold, 'having real pity for him and her'. And when, some months later, he heard news of them, he remarked characteristically: 'I could be willing to do something for them, were I not sure to bring them over again hither.'

Mrs. Pepys's brother, Balthazar (Balty) St. Michel, desired, and seemed sometimes to deserve, the interposition of his patronage. He managed to secure for him a post of Muster-master. 'He is mighty glad of it, and earnest to fit himself for it, but I do find, poor man, that he is troubled how to dispose of his wife, and apparently it is out of fear of her and his honour, and I believe he hath received some cause of this his jealousy and care, and I do pity him for it, and will endeavour to find out some way to do it for him.' Balty, largely through Pepys's influence, advanced in the scale of naval appointments, and eventually became Special Commissioner for the Navy.

The affection Pepys had for his father was exceptional, in its strength and endurance. Soon after he obtained his appointment on the Navy Board his father retired from his business as tailor and resided at the family house at Brampton. He made, however, fairly frequent visits to London, and was always given a very genuine welcome by his son. He was not well off, and was grateful to Pepys for financial assistance from time to time. When Pepys promised to add £30 a year to his income the old man 'was overjoyed and wept'. 'This discourse ended to the joy of my father and no less to me to see that I am able to do this.' A few days later he gave him money to buy a horse, as well as about £23 for various expenses 'which the poor man takes with infinite kindnesse, and I do not think I can bestow it better'.

A year later his father had been suffering acute pain from a long-standing rupture; and Pepys was anxious to do something for his relief. 'I long to have him in town, that I may see what can be done for him here; for I would fain do all I can that I may have him live, and take pleasure in my doing well in the world.' When his father arrived in town, and had put off his travelling-clothes, he looked 'mighty spruce, and I love to see him cheerful'. He found that 'the poor man's patience under it [the pain] and his good heart and humour, as soon as he was out of it, did so work upon me, that my heart was sad to think upon his condition, but do hope that a way will be found by a steel truss to relieve him'. This hope was, happily, satisfied.

The association between Pepys and his brothers was much less pleasant. Thomas, the elder, succeeded to his father's business as tailor. He became lax and unprincipled, and died in wretched circumstances. John, the younger, was of a scholarly turn, but seemed to lack application. When he was at Cambridge, Pepys, who was paying his expenses, felt it necessary to give him 'a most severe reprimand for his bad account he gives me of his studies. This I did with great passion and sharp words, which I was sorry to be forced to say. . . . I was sorry to see him give me no answer, but, for aught I see, to hear me without great resentment, and such as I should have had in his condition. But I have done my duty, let him do his, for I am resolved to be as good as my word.'

When Pepys looked over Thomas's papers after his death he found, to his great anger, several letters from his brother, John, 'speaking very foule words of me . . . which I am very glad to know, and shall make him repent them'. Two days later the wretched John had to listen while Pepys read the 'roguish letters' to their father. Pepys pronounced that he would not make John any further monetary allowance 'and other words very severe, while he, like a simple rogue, made very silly and churlish answers to me, not like a man of any goodness and wit, at which I was as much disturbed as the other, and will be as good as my word in making him to his cost know that I will remember his carriage to me in this particular the longest day I live'.

Many months afterwards, on his mother's leaving London after a visit, Pepys gave her some money 'and took kind leave of her, she, poor wretch, desiring that I would forgive my brother, John, but I refused it her, which troubled her, poor soul, but I did it in kind words, and so let the discourse go off, she leaving me though in a great deal of sorrow'.

More than two years after the discovery of the mischievous

letters Pepys mentioned that he had written a letter to John, 'the first I have done since my being angry with him, and that so sharpe a one too that I was sorry almost to send it when I had wrote it, but it is preparatory to my being kind to him, and sending for him up hither when he hath passed his degree of Master of Arts'. Soon he wrote to his father saying that if John proved good for anything he would probably arrange to get him preferment. When, in due course, John came to stay with Pepys in London, he appeared to be such a good-natured, harmless young man that Mrs. Pepys took a liking to him, and Pepys admitted that he began to 'fancy him'.

Later, John took orders; but, in process of time, he changed his profession, on obtaining valuable public offices through Pepys's influence. Unfortunately he was, it would seem, inadequately equipped with the qualities requisite to undertake important administrative posts. Here Pepys's kindness outran his concern for the general interest. It would have been better if he had treated John more understandingly in the period after the sad episode of the discovered letters. His protracted vindictiveness at that time reveals an unpleasant aspect of his character; and it is difficult to avoid the conclusion that, there, he had the appearance of being a bully. He as good as admitted that if John had stood up to him, and protested that too much was being made of a passing indiscretion, he would have relented.

One or two incidents in his dealings with Sir W. Penn suggest rancour; but, on the whole, they do not seem to amount to more than passing expressions of exasperation. He often made indignant remarks about Penn which had only momentary significance. 'I find him much out of humour, so that I do not think matters go well with him, and I am glad of it.' This was the result of a not very amicable discussion. He could use some such expression as 'I shall remember him for a knave while I live'. These choleric outbursts are by no means to be taken literally. They were the quick effect of some remark which seemed to belittle his status or prestige, subjects on which he felt strongly.

He also denounced another Navy Commissioner (Pett) and threatened him, in the Diary only, with his displeasure. He was, for a brief time, indignant because Pett had questioned his efficiency. 'Commissioner Pett did let fall several scurvy words concerning my pretending to know masts as well as any body, which I know proceeds ever since I told him I could measure a piece of timber as well as any body employed by the King. But, however, I shall remember him for a black sheep again a good while, with all his fair words to me . . .' This animosity is to be explained by the rivalry between the life-long technician and the aspiring amateur. Their social relations had been excellent; but when Pepys was touched on the raw, he could be waspish. The resentment was doubtless soon forgotten.

If we take a broad view of the Diary, we may easily be assured that Pepys was essentially good-humoured. But his unmitigated frankness is such that he occasionally reveals himself as possessing the unpleasant qualities of irascibility and vindictiveness. His descriptions of these infrequent occurrences are so lively that they stand out from the narrative, and stamp themselves on the reader's recollection. Admirable but unobtrusive features such as benignity, being treated by him in a cursory manner, are easily disregarded; and, as they are relatively lacking in incident, they can fail to be placed to the writer's credit. No doubt Pepys was so intent on being truthful and accurate in composing the Diary that he neglected to consider the ambiguous impression of himself that he was creating. The scrupulous investigator must surely decide that, in spite of occasional instances of harshness, his kindness plainly predominates.

14

Capricious Husband: Appreciative and Critical

It is inevitable, from the peculiar kind of frankness with which the Diary is written, that we gain a more lively impression of the clashes and dissensions in Pepys's marriage than its smooth passages. Many writers commenting on this topic are satisfied that he and Elizabeth were genuinely fond of each other throughout their life together. He had sufficient vitality to enable him to be in love with his wife and with other women at the same time; and she was constant in matrimony largely because she was intensely proud of her clever and prosperous husband. But they were not well suited to be partners in marriage. He was too efficient and exacting for a woman of her temperament. She was inclined to be shallow, and would, we may guess, have liked to have indulged in a good deal of frivolity mixed with harmless sentimentalism, if she had had the opportunity. It is pretty clear that she had had but scanty education of a formal kind, whereas Pepys had been able to take considerable advantage of a sound schooling and a University training. As a result there was a limit to the subjects which they could discuss with mutual pleasure. Elizabeth was, moreover, lacking in competence as a housewife, a serious defect in Pepys's eyes. Equally serious perhaps, in view of her husband's disposition, was her lack of musical ability. If they had had the bond of music to unite them, they might have avoided most of the conflicts that disfigured their married life. The bond of children would have been even more effective.

No doubt Pepys married Elizabeth because she was beautiful. Acting with the excitability characteristic of him, he overlooked the importance of more serviceable qualities. His admiration of her physical charms is undoubted. Early in the Diary, when mentioning a genteel wedding reception, he remarked: 'But among all the beauties there, my wife was thought the greatest.' A little later he secured the entrée of his wife and himself to the Queen's presence-chamber. He considered the Princess Henrietta to be very pretty. 'But my wife standing near her with two or three black patches on, and well dressed, did seem to me much handsomer than she.'

Pepys, though he often preferred more witty companions, enjoyed her company. When she went into the country on a visit, and left her husband in London, he almost invariably expressed himself as sad at her absence. Once he said that he was 'grieved in my heart to part with my wife, being worse by much without her'. On going to bed that night, he felt 'very lonely'. He could say 'all things, methinks, melancholy in the absence of my wife', and 'sad for want of my wife, whom I love with all my heart, though of late she has given me some troubled thoughts'. He was generally glad to see her back, with such a remark as 'merry and glad to see my poor wife'. But her unexpected arrival might not be convenient. 'Anon comes home my wife from Brampton, not looked for till Saturday, which will hinder me of a little pleasure, but I am glad of her coming.'

He appreciated her shrewdness and common sense. Occasionally, he consulted her about his financial position. When he was in bad odour with the Earl of Sandwich, owing to his well-meant but unlucky letter of protest about the Earl's personal behaviour, he explained to Elizabeth that his patron owed him £700, and that he was exercised in his mind how he should behave. She gave him 'very good and rational advice' on this subject. He was to be haughty with Sandwich's entourage, 'slighting every body but my Lord and Lady', and to dress richly and modishly when he visited the house. The problem of preserving his estate induced him to consult her in an emergency. The situation of the nation, at the time of the threat from the Dutch fleet in 1667, seemed to portend something like disaster. Pepys was considering whether he ought to move some of his gold coin from his house into the country; and he discussed with his father and Elizabeth the best course to take. In the following year, just before he had to make his great defence of the Navy Board before the House of Commons, he could not sleep in bed, and got his wife 'to talk to me to comfort me', which she did, and told him that he should not feel himself tied to an office which put too great a strain on him. In awkward predicaments of a minor kind also he found encouragement and relief in just telling Elizabeth the facts. He had, for instance, a stiff and unpleasant argument with his friend, Creed. But after he had unburdened himself to his wife, 'my head and heart was mightily lighter than they were before . . .'

It was not until he had reason to fear that he might lose his wife's affection that he came to a whole-hearted realization how much he was attached to her, and how much he relied on her. This was the state of affairs after the lamentable occasion when he was caught kissing and embracing Deb Willet. On driving out with Elizabeth in their coach, he had 'now little pleasure to look about me to see the fine faces, for fear of displeasing my wife, [in] whom I take great comfort now, more than ever, in pleasing; and it is a real joy to me'. He had, at that time, to be specially careful to avoid intensifying Elizabeth's jealousy of Mrs. Knepp, Pepys's actress friend. When he was at the King's Playhouse with Elizabeth, 'Knepp looked upon us, but I durst not show her any countenance . . .' Again, at church, he felt a glow of pleasure at the entry of the milliner's engaging wife, 'but I durst not to be seen to mind her for fear of my wife's seeing me, though the woman I did never speak twenty words to . . .'

Some weeks later he remarked that there was 'much kindness between me and my wife, which, now-a-days is all my care'. But Elizabeth's jealousy of Deb kept breaking out anew. She even accused him of dreaming of Deb, as if this was a matter under his control! She suspected that Pepys was still seeing the girl; and she had heard that she was being maligned by her. With much trouble Pepys pacified his wife. 'I did at last bring her to very good and kind terms, poor heart! and I was heartily glad of it, for I do see there is no man can be happier than myself, if I will, with her.'

Often, in his married life, he alternated between alarm at her possible displeasure and a considerable disregard for her welfare. Sometimes these sentiments seem almost to have coexisted. One winter's afternoon he had taken Betty Michell out on a jaunt which was so extended that he was afraid it might be discovered by Elizabeth. He was 'in a sweat', for the situation was 'the worst in reference à my femme that ever I was in in my life'. He was obviously in great trepidation at his reception in case his wife had learnt what had happened. More than once he was afraid of his wife's discovering that he had been to the theatre without her. But, at the same time, he was spending much of his leisure regardless of her need for diversion. This contradictory behaviour may be explained by a principle that often guided him: the most serious indiscretion is to be found out.

In contrast with his frequently expressed satisfaction in his companionship with his wife, he mentioned numerous grounds for discontent. His not infrequent objections to her 'sluttery' are likely to have been justified, though not his way of expressing his disapprobation. She was untidy. Clothes were left lying about. This made him angry; but he usually soon regretted making a scene. Sometimes Elizabeth failed to see that the house was kept properly clean, though Pepys was so fond of having improvements and alterations made in the house that the task of the maids must have often been difficult. The cooking was not always to his taste; but she could not be expected to ensure that all her cooks were competent. He might have taken more philosophically than he did the meat being blackened, or a rabbit being only half roasted. Elizabeth lacked an essential quality of a housewife: she forgot things she ought to have remembered. Pepys remarked, in a manner typical of him: 'I am a little vexed to see that she do not retain things in her memory that belong to the house as she ought and I myself do . . .' (But he himself was far from perfect in this respect.) Moreover, she was not a good manager. When there was to be a dinner- or supper-party, she was sometimes found lacking in adequate preparation.

A good deal of Elizabeth's lack of efficiency in running her house was due to her excessive familiarity with her maids. She was driven to associate with them unduly, chiefly owing to Pepys's failure to see that she had sufficient opportunities for social activity and for recreation. She thus spoiled the maids, who became cheeky and undisciplined. As a result, efficiency suffered; or she quarrelled with them, and gave them notice.

Troubles such as these were intensified when young female companions were introduced into the household to keep Elizabeth company. She generally became jealous of them; and the home suffered from an air of irritability and discontent. But the companions could, as in the case of Ashwell, serve Elizabeth's purpose very well. When Pepys became ridiculously jealous of Elizabeth's dancing-master, she found that she could be scornful and even insolent to him on this subject if Ashwell were present, for he could not take her to task on such a subject before the companion. There was not much that he could do about this; and he became increasingly infuriated at Elizabeth's arrogance and undisciplined manner. 'I do see great cause every day to curse the time that ever I did give way to the taking of a woman for her, though I could never have a better [than Ashwell], and also the letting of her learn to dance, by both which her mind is so devilishly taken off her business and minding her occasions, and besides has got such an opinion in her of my being jealous, that it is never to be removed, I fear, nor hardly my trouble that attends it; but I must have patience.'

At last, he sent her away into the country with some slight hope that their dissensions would be forgotten. He ruminated over these problems when left alone in London. 'I fear I shall find a trouble of my wife when she comes home to get down her head again . . .' And he concluded that 'this heighth that my wife is come to' was 'occasioned from my own folly in giving her too much head heretofore for the year past'. He used the same metaphor when Elizabeth returned to London. 'I find that my wife has got too great head to be brought down soon . . .' The fact was that Pepys only seemed able to keep her under the sort of control he desired if she were left to live a solitary life at home; and that situation often led to trouble, for she naturally rebelled against a miserably dull existence. Three years after the episode of the dancing-master, when Elizabeth was staying away from home, at Woolwich, because of the disorganization caused by the Great Fire, he visited her, 'and there find my wife out of humour and indifferent, as she uses upon her having much liberty abroad'. Again, two years later, he found that Elizabeth's sojourn in the country had once more had unfortunate effects on her manner towards him. 'Somewhat out of humour all day, reflecting on my wife's neglect of things, and impertinent humour got by this liberty of being from me, which she is never to be trusted with; for she is a fool.'

He could make remarks like this when exasperated, and he could be sweeping in his condemnation. But it would be a profound mistake to consider that he meant exactly what he said. Nevertheless, he partly did; and it is in this way that he should be interpreted. After a quite trivial altercation with Elizabeth over a question of the payment of a maid's wages, he confided to himself that he was 'cruelly vexed in my mind that all my trouble in this world almost should arise from my disorders in my family and the indiscretion of a wife that brings me nothing almost (besides a comely person) but only trouble and discontent'. This is a patent exaggeration; but, even if much modified, it has some significance. Taken by themselves, such statements would imply that the marriage was near breaking-point. But it was far from that. These forlorn lamentations are the impulsive outbreaks of a kind that Pepys could indulge in when peevish and perverse. If they are read in conjunction with the more genial and sincerely affectionate remarks already quoted, in which he declares his deeply-felt happiness with his wife, a considerable amount of qualification is required.

When he referred to her in varying circumstances as 'my poor wife', he may easily be misapprehended. The phrase may seem to imply a slight degree of contempt. Sometimes in the Diary the word 'poor' as applied to Elizabeth is evidently meant to convey the idea that he was sorry for her because, for instance, she had been hard at work in the home. But at other times it is probably an indication of tenderness. Some dictionaries recognize this as an occasional usage. We might say today 'my little wife'. This would fit in with such phrases in the Diary as 'merry and glad to see my poor wife', and 'my poor wife, who gives me more and more content'.

He was also in the habit of describing her as 'the poor wretch', which might be thought to signify disparagement. But it seems that he was usually professing compassion. The 'poor wretch' was troubled with her lonely life, or was in pain on the unfortunate occasions when he pulled her nose, and when he struck her in the eye. The expression was also used by him when she was in pain due to illness. He was glad that she should have her collection of jewellery, 'for it is fit the wretch should have something to content herself with'. As we shall notice, he was not always considerate to her. At the same time, he often pitied her because she was not happy, or because she was physically tired, or ill. But it can certainly be asserted that he never felt contempt for her; and words like 'poor' and 'wretch' can give this impression.

Sufficient proof that the expression 'poor wretch' could be used by him in a compassionate sense, without any implication of contempt, is found in his mention of Lady Sandwich in these terms at a time when she was suffering from the measles. A century or so later someone would, perhaps, have tried to convey the same meaning by referring to 'the poor creature'.

15

Capricious Husband: Amiable and Choleric

Although in some respects Pepys was neglectful of Elizabeth, he never failed in compassion and practical sympathy when she was unmistakably in need of them. When she was ill, and this happened frequently, he was always prepared to spend time sitting with her, or having a meal by her bedside, or diverting her by reading, or in some other manner. One year he had his Christmas dinner with her in her bedroom 'with great content'; and after dinner sat talking with her a good while. There are several such entries as: 'Kept her bed all day, and I up and dined by her bedside.' When she had been very ill with diarrhoea and vomiting, he lay for a while on the bed with her so as to aid her all he could. In such circumstances, he would sometimes sit with her and 'pity her'. He even went home specially in order to comfort her after she had had a tooth extracted. All these items add up to a convincing sum.

He would also comfort her in distresses that were not physical, but which nevertheless called for tender sympathy. Although she seems to have been consistently faithful to her husband in the sense of never having serious affairs with men, she was sentimental, and enjoyed the admiration of male friends. A brief friendship with a Mr. (later Sir Henry) Sheres, which had given her intense pleasure, ended on his returning to Tangier. After a final meeting, she was out of humour all the evening; and Pepys was vexed in case she might have too lively a concern for Sheres, whose aptitude for poetry and sympathetic disposition had aroused Elizabeth's particular interest. They went to bed; but she 'did not rest almost all the night, so as in the night I was forced to take her and hug her to put her to rest'. This delightful little story puts Pepys in a very favourable light. He overcame his slight suspicions and his incipient jealousy; and, forgetting about himself, tried to soothe and console his wife.

Quite frequently he gave presents to Elizabeth: seldom to celebrate occasions, or the acceptable ones which have no rationale, given just because the giver wanted to give them. Some were articles of dress which were necessary in the absence of a dress allowance. Others were given to smooth over a fracas, or to quiet his conscience after he had behaved to her in a regrettable manner. But circumstances could prompt him to be bountiful. There was an occasion when he seems to have acted with notable generosity at a time when he could hardly afford an expensive present. 'In the evening my wife being a little impatient I went along with her to buy her a necklace of pearl, which will cost £4. 10s., which I am willing to comply with her in for her encouragement, and because I have lately got money, having now above £200 in cash beforehand in the world.' Considering that Pepys at that time was endeavouring to set up a creditably furnished house, and also to have some money at his back in case of need, this gift was worth more than the sum it cost.

But Pepys was versatile; and, in spite of his being habitually kind, and often revealing himself as tender-hearted, he had, as we have seen, a quick temper. It was part of his excitability. He enjoyed good living, and was sometimes given ample occasion for being angry by having an overdone or underdone dish set in front of him. Quite small matters could produce an undue reaction. The sauce for a leg of mutton was sweet, so he refused to eat the mutton, and made himself a martyr by dining off the marrow-bone. It was even more aggravating for him when a badly cooked dinner was provided for an important guest. When Sir William Coventry was invited to dinner both the leg of mutton and the capons were underdone. He tried to make the best of the situation; but, when the guest had gone, he was 'very angry with my wife and people'.

The indifferent management of the house by Elizabeth was also a frequent cause of displays of temper; the dog fouling the house, the servants being allowed to be out late at night, or the rooms left in a dirty condition, caused him to flare up. He could, in such circumstances, be violent, and his uncontrolled behaviour must have caused considerable alarm in the household. The mere fact of some untidiness provoked him to kick a fine basket, a present from him to his wife, and ruin it. And the even less important incident of a crumpled tablecloth induced prodigious and preposterous commotion. 'I grew angry and flung the trenchers about the room, and in a mighty heat I was: so a clean cloth was laid, and my poor wife very patient . . .' In this and other instances of his dubious behaviour he subsequently, in the Diary, managed to view the scene objectively; and this quality has an extenuating effect.

He prided himself on being a great manager, and liked to keep Elizabeth's activities under close control. His interferences regarding her manner of dress must have been particularly aggravating. When she had, for instance, dressed herself for a christening, 'I took occasion to fall out with my wife, very highly about her ribbands being ill-matched and of two colours, and to very high words, so that, like a passionate fool, I did call her whore, for which I was afterwards sorry'. He evidently regarded himself as being entitled to disapprove of his wife's clothes, and to refuse to go out with her if she was not dressed to his liking. A blue petticoat, i.e. skirt, seemed to him 'a silly dress', and he was cross about it; but it turned out that he was merely peevish because he was hungry. She would even be so compliant as to ask him to direct her what gown to put on, if he had expressed dissatisfaction with her first attempt. But once when they were on the way to church together he became angry because she was not dressed 'as I would have her'. She was naturally indignant, and returned home.

He expected from his wife not only compliance but submissiveness; and little infuriated him more than a lack of deference. His imperious behaviour subjected her to considerable strains; and, being a woman of spirit, she was sometimes unmistakably insubordinate. When taunted with being a bad housewife, she called him 'pricklouse'. He was not the man to suffer such scoffs without retaliation. Once, when she answered him back, he stupidly pulled her nose and hurt her; and he had to buy her 'a pretty silke for a petticoat' to quieten her down. It was worse still when she gave him 'some cross answer' on his complaining about her failure to control her servants properly, for he struck her such a blow over the left eye 'as the poor wretch did cry out and was in great pain, but yet her spirit was such as to endeavour to bite and scratch me. But I coying [toying] with her made her leave crying, and sent for butter and parsley, and friends presently with one another . . .'

Generally these displays of temper were over at once; and he regained control of himself. But if she charged him with consistent lack of consideration he could be implacable. Her long-nurtured resentment against him for compelling her to lead a lonely life induced her to write to him a formal letter of protest. His agitation on reading this letter incited him to the heartless destruction of many of her private papers. In addition, he would not be friends with her for some time. It is probable that his sustained anger was largely due to his apprehensiveness that the letter, which had been left about by a strange accident, might have been seen by others, and his reputation as a husband disparaged, a subject on which he was highly susceptible.

Among Pepys's various defects of character, few are at the same time more inglorious and ludicrous than his jealousy of his wife's male acquaintances. With no real provocation, he made himself miserable, and he imperilled his happiness with his wife. And this behaviour was all the more reprehensible because he was so frequently unfaithful to her.

Early in the period of the Diary he suspected some old admirers of Elizabeth of having designs on her affections. There was a son of Lord John Somerset whom she had met in France. Pepys showed him 'no great countenance, to avoyd further acquaintance'. But this young man gave Elizabeth a bracelet of rings, 'which did a little trouble me, though I knew there was no hurt in it yet, but only for fear of further acquaintance'. Later there seemed to be some secret appointment made through a French footman. But there was never the least evidence of any irregularity in this or in any other of her supposed affairs. Major Holmes, with his gold-laced suit, seemed to be making advances, 'at which I was troubled because of the old business which he attempted upon my wife'. Captain Ferrers, too, had, he heard, been so kind to her at Brampton 'that I perceive I have some jealousy of him, but I know what is the Captain's manner of carriage, and therefore it is nothing to me'.

Every reader of the Diary has delighted in the absurdity of the figure cut by Pepys in the protracted jealousy he experienced in regard to Pembleton, his wife's dancing-master, whom he described as 'a pretty neat black [i.e. dark-headed] man, but married'. At first he was 'a little angry with my wife for minding nothing now but the dancing-master, having him come twice a day, which is folly'. But soon he was in the exasperating situation of being wildly jealous, and at the same time suspecting that he was acting without any real justification. Arriving home late one evening, he 'found it almost night, and my wife and the dancing-master alone above, not dancing but talking. Now so deadly full of jealousy I am that my heart and head did so cast about and fret that I could not do any business possibly. . . But it is a deadly folly and plague that I bring upon myself to be so jealous . . .'

For many weeks to come he allowed himself to be tormented by misgivings. Pembleton took her hand when playing at nine-pins; he leered upon her in church during the sermon, or so it seemed to Pepys. Small and completely harmless circumstances suggested guilt. Then he would reprove himself, and try to believe that his suspicions were baseless. Once more his jealousy flared up in terrific intensity. There was, he concluded, 'something more than ordinary between my wife and him, which do so trouble me that I know not at this very minute that I now write this almost what either I write or am doing, nor how to carry myself to my wife in it . . . This is my devilish jealousy, which I pray God may be false, but it makes a very hell in my mind, which the God of heaven remove, or I shall be very unhappy.'

It was only natural that Elizabeth felt strongly that, by his lack of confidence in her, he was behaving in an insulting way; and she tried to make him feel small. She taunted him in front of Ashwell, her companion, so that his folly might easily be bruited abroad. He could say nothing. One day she told him before Ashwell that Pembleton had called, but she would not let him come in unless Pepys was there, which made him ashamed of himself. He richly deserved to be humiliated.

Even some weeks after the dancing-classes were over any reminder of Pembleton put him into an extraordinary state of agitation. Seeing him in the Park, as he thought, 'my blood did rise in my face, and I fell into a sweat from my old jealousy and hate'. Elizabeth was not with him on this occasion. But when he was in church with her a little later he saw Pembleton. 'Which, Lord! into what a sweat did it put me! . . . But it makes me mad to see of what a jealous temper I am and cannot helpe it . . .' This behaviour was not that of a normal man, or anything like it.

There were several other instances of the same infirmity, but it is not necessary to do more than give some names and briefest particulars. Incredible as it may seem, Pepys actually had some suspicions of his faithful and completely virtuous assistant, Will Hewer. Elizabeth sometimes sent for Will for some entirely innocent purpose. Pepys once said: 'But, Lord! why should I think any evil of that; and yet I cannot forbear it.' The extent of his incomprehensible derangement on this subject is best illustrated by the incident when Elizabeth complained to him that Will had been in the house and had been chattering with the maids. He actually suspected that Elizabeth had plotted to invite Will to see her at a time when she knew that he would be out on business. It is difficult to see how he could suspect her of such a plot, when she herself brought the subject to his notice. He tried to pull himself together, and to see things in a reasonable light. 'But this cursed humour I cannot cool in myself by all the reason I have, which God forgive me for, and convince me of the folly of it, and the disquiet it brings me.' So extravagant was his jealous behaviour that it seems to resemble that of some distorted character in an Elizabethan tragedy.

Other disturbers of Pepys's peace of mind were the son of Sir W. Penn, afterwards the famous Quaker, and a Mr. Coleman, a young Guardsman, who, according to a sly friend of Pepys's, was a rogue for women. Although these two gentlemen were radically different in type, they were both, we may be sure, entirely innocent of any desire to capture Elizabeth's affections. Further names could be added to the list. Moreover, matters reached such a ridiculous pass that, when Pepys was to be out of town for a day, he was tortured in his mind from jealousy, surmising that his wife might be courted by some entirely imaginary person, 'which', as he admitted, 'is a hell to my mind, and yet without all reason'. There seemed to be no means of curing anyone so utterly irrational.

A scheme devised by Elizabeth may have had some effect in checking the intemperance of his suspicions. He arrived home one day 'thinking to be merry' and 'was vexed with my wife's having looked out a letter in Sir Philip Sidney about jealousy for me to read, which she industriously and maliciously caused me to do, and the truth is my conscience told me it was most proper for me, and therefore was touched at it, but took no notice of it, but read it out most frankly, but it stuck in my stomach'. He can hardly have believed that Elizabeth was so simple as to be taken in by this obvious piece of play-acting. At last, perhaps, he would realize what a perennial fool he had been making of himself, for she had found a way to make him feel ridiculous.

16

Capricious Husband: Sometimes Implacable

There can surely be no published diary that includes a larger number of descriptions of quarrels between husband and wife than Pepys's. The descriptions, which are often most vivid, have a special interest in that they sometimes disclose who was the more conciliatory, and who the more implacable. It may be said at once that, while both could be conciliatory, Elizabeth was much the more so. Pepys was sometimes implacable, but Elizabeth rarely.

When a quarrel was quickly healed it was more often than not Elizabeth who took the initiative. On their falling out, one day at dinner, over their opinions of the competence of the maids, Pepys went off to his study 'in a discontent'. 'After dinner my wife comes up to me [i.e. upstairs to his study] and all friends again . . .' She was plainly the peacemaker. Likewise: 'Up by and by my wife comes and good friends again . . .' And: '. . . so being good friends again, my wife seeking it . . .' One afternoon they quarrelled because Elizabeth accused him of giving her insufficient liberty. After supper Pepys, obviously in a pet, went off to bed. 'My wife made great means to be friends, coming to my bedside and doing all things to please me, and at last I could not hold out, but seemed pleased . . .'

Elizabeth was, with some justification, jealous of Pepys's admiration of Mrs. Pierce and Mrs. Knepp; and when, on one of several such occasions, she called them disparaging names, there was a sharp conflict. She insisted on his taking her for a drive, presumably so that she could feel that she was being paid proper attention. He was mum and glum; but she soon made advances, 'leaning on me as desirous to be friends'. Perhaps the most impressive instance of Elizabeth's notable capacity for forgiveness was that of his striking her over the eye, to which reference has already been made. In a few hours, though disfigured and still suffering, he described her as 'in a very good temper to me'.

These selected examples are sufficient to constitute an imposing testimony of Elizabeth's amiability. Pepys's record is much less admirable. There are only one or two instances of his seeming to take the initiative in composing a quarrel. They had 'very high words' about the perpetually troublesome subject of the merits of one of their maids, during which she called him 'perfidious and man of no conscience . . . but I tempered myself very well, so that though we went to bed with discontent she yielded to me and began to be fond so that being willing myself to peace, we did before sleep become very good friends'. Sometimes he showed restraint when he might have pretended that he was in the right. In such circumstances he would make such assertions as: 'I took no notice of it at all, but fell to other discourse', or 'I beginning to practice more temper, and to give her her way . . .' Elizabeth had right on her side in her grievance about the attentions Pepys paid to Mrs. Pierce and Mrs. Knepp; but she put herself in the wrong when she called them 'wenches'. Pepys curbed himself at one of these outbursts, as he saw the wisdom of moderation. 'I did give her no words to offend her, and quietly let all pass, and so to bed without any good looke or words to or from my wife.' Incidents like this are hardly proof of his having the qualities of a positive peacemaker. He did no more than hope that, as a result of his inaction, disquiets would be allayed. He was not prepared to wield the olive branch.

There are, alas, several occasions when it was largely Pepys's fault that he and his wife went to bed without having made up their quarrel and become friends again. He could sulk; and his obstinate sullenness sometimes persisted in a way which suggests a more unpleasant character than that of a man who is merely quick-tempered. It happened one day that Elizabeth had gone out he knew not whither; and he evidently suspected that she had an assignation with young Somerset. When he came home in the evening she had long since returned, 'but I seemed very angry, as indeed I am, and did not all night show her any countenance, neither before nor in bed, and so slept and rose discontented'. This was an especially bad case, for he went to bed 'still in discontent' the next night. Both were to blame. Elizabeth should not have been secretive. He should not have been jealous and suspicious without any ground. It looks as if the main responsibility was on him.

He was particularly touchy, doubtless because of a guilty conscience, when Elizabeth took a strong line about the lonely life she led. She had been forming schemes for employing a girl companion without consulting him. This angered him; and on the following evening he came home to supper, 'and there was very sullen to my wife, and so went to bed and to sleep (though with much ado, my mind being troubled) without speaking one word to her'.

Another cause of dissension between them, of which more must be said later, was his attempt to control his wife in her expenditure on dress and suchlike. He took the strongest exception to her buying a pair of pendants for her ears without his consent. This 'did vex me and brought both me and her to very high and very foule words from her to me [sic], such as trouble me to think she should have in her mouth, and reflecting upon our old differences, which I hate to have remembered. I vowed to break them [the pendants], or that she should go and get what she could for them again. I went with that resolution out of doors; the poor wretch afterwards in a little while did send out to change them for her money again. I followed Besse her messenger at the 'Change, and there did consult and sent her back; I would not have them changed, being satisfied that she yielded. So I went home, and friends again as to that business; but the words I could not get out of my mind, and so went to bed at night discontented, and she came to bed with me, but all would not make me friends, but sleep and rise in the morning angry.' Here again, it was evidently his sense of guilt, in regard to their old

differences, that was the chief explanation of his implacability. He
could not bear to be shown up.

It seems astounding that another ground for a full-dress quarrel
was Elizabeth's buying 'a laced handkercher and pinner' without
his leave; and it is equally astounding that their squabble, for it does
not merit a more serious description, was not composed at the end
of the day. They 'so continued till bed, and did not sleep friends'.

Love of money was certainly the explanation of some of his
sustained anger. He managed to lash himself into a painful degree of
wrath in connexion with the burying of his gold coin in the country
after the Dutch fleet had forced its way up the Medway. His
wife 'did give me so bad an account of her and my father's
method of burying of our gold, that made me mad: and she herself
is not pleased with it . . .' The work was done in open daylight in
a place which was overlooked by neighbours. 'Such was my trouble
at this, that I did not sup with her, nor speak to her to-night, but
to bed and sleep.' It is easily understandable that he should be
deeply disturbed at the prospect of losing some of his hardly earned
money; but to harbour ill will to the extent he did was insensate.

When he went himself into the country at a later date to recover
the gold he was infuriated because at first the site could not be
located, and then because the bag was broken, the coins scattered,
and about a hundred of them missing, 'which did make me mad'.
He should have entrusted the work to more competent hands.

His methods of quieting her, when her grievances induced her to
inveigh against him, were sometimes effective; but they were
hardly defensible. One was to affect to be engaged in business.
Another was to pretend to fall asleep. An unamiable one was to take
no notice of what she said, 'thinking that will be the best way, and
let it wear away itself'. Even more insufferable was his behaviour
after they had had 'high words' about his interference with her
manner of dress. 'I fell to read a book (Boyle's Hydrostatics) aloud
in my chamber and let her talk till she was tired and vexed that I
would not hear her, and so became friends . . .' Elizabeth's good
nature must have deceived him into thinking that good relations
could be re-established by such brutal tactics. It is surprising that

she did not find some way of insisting that he listened to her complaints.

In view of the frequency of Pepys's provocations, it would be strange if Elizabeth had not been goaded at some time into behaving in an altogether unpardonable manner. On a famous occasion, her resentment was so passionate that she, who was ordinarily eager to maintain goodwill, appeared in the role of assailant. She had been for many days nursing the idea that Pepys might break his word, see Deb again, and be unfaithful. She had some slight, but inaccurate report of a meeting. Her fury mounted. She refused to come to bed, and made up the fire, sitting brooding for hours. Finally, she opened the curtains of their bed and made to attack her husband with tongs red-hot at the ends. Pepys leapt out of bed, and she dropped the tongs. The menace of Deb had so worked upon her sensibilities that ordinary standards are inapplicable to this behaviour. She would not have been human if she had never been so much exasperated as to exceed the limits of legitimate protest.

17

Plans for His Wife's Contentment

In his early days in Seething Lane, Pepys seems to have felt but little responsibility for seeing that his wife had opportunities for enjoying company and recreation. She occasionally visited her relations, or his, in other parts of London for an hour or two; and they came to see her. Before long, she was kindly treated by Lady Sandwich, and was encouraged to call on her from time to time. These calls were often protracted, and, it seems, a source of considerable pleasure. But more was needed to ensure her well-being.

At this period Pepys was constantly engaged in social activities, especially dinner-parties and drinking-parties; and he often went to the play, either by himself or with a friend or friends, scarcely ever taking Elizabeth with him. This gross neglect is difficult to explain. He seems to have thought that she would be best at home, out of danger perhaps of being led astray, or of getting fine ideas. His aim may well have been for her to be satisfied in her domestic work, and in controlling her maid or maids. There was a good deal to do in the newly occupied house.

Pepys kept a careful and accurate record of his visits to the play, and of his companions there, if any. He started playgoing in earnest in the winter of 1660; and, from that time up to the middle of the summer of 1661, the figures he gives, when analysed, are most revealing. In that period, he went to the play twenty-five times by himself, sixteen times with friends; and only once did he take his wife. The situation naturally mounted to a crisis. About the middle of 1661 Elizabeth rebelled. It is surprising that she did not do so before. As a result of this exigency, Pepys had to swear to Elizabeth that he would never go to a play without her. He did not by any means adhere to this undertaking; but, from the time of this oath onwards, the record was much more creditable. In the second half of 1661 he went ten times alone, eleven times with friends, and sixteen times with his wife. This oath was still considered to be operative in the following year; and, as he had then been seen at the play alone by Sir W. Penn, he was a good deal troubled that he would be bound to confess to Elizabeth that he had broken his undertaking.

For some three or four years after this he did not indulge in playgoing at all extensively, largely because he was immersed in his professional work. But the tension between him and his wife that arose in the periods just mentioned became evident again in 1668. While Elizabeth had been away in the country during the early summer Pepys took the opportunity of enjoying a spate of playgoing. When she returned she was angry at discovering what had happened; and he tried to make up for his indiscretion by taking her to the play a number of times.

As a means of family entertainment, he liked to organize excursions to parks and to the country near London. A party on the river was an occasional alternative. Often, especially after he had accumulated a good deal of money, he delighted in arranging a drive in a coach in an easterly direction 'to take the ayre', to stay and walk in the fields, to sit and enjoy a picnic, or to visit an inn and partake of such refreshment as cakes and wine. Shorter coach drives were taken to Moorfields, Bow, Whitechapel, Shoreditch, and Mile End. A frequently repeated longer one was what he called their 'grand' tour, by Hackney, Kingsland, Newington Green to Islington, where the famous cheese cakes tempted them.

They sometimes proceeded to their destination by water, or stayed for a time on the water, going to Greenwich, Gravesend, Jamaica House (for the tea-gardens at Bermondsey), or, in the other direction, to Mortlake, Barn Elms, Wandsworth, Putney, and Fulham.

The famous gardens at 'Foxhall' (Vauxhall) provided another pleasant resort that they could frequent. Sometimes he went there with a male companion only, or with a mixed party of friends, but more often with Elizabeth and her woman companion. One or two of their maids occasionally accompanied them. At Vauxhall Gardens they could have refreshment, listen to music, enjoy humorous entertainment, or watch the gallants of the town. Once, when Pepys took two maids and the boy, as well as his wife, the maids gathered pinks, and the boy crept through the hedge and picked 'abundance of roses'. The maids could also amuse themselves by running races. Pepys was not a spoilsport on these occasions; on the contrary he was gay and sprightly, though prudent in expenditure. At the old Garden he found the food very expensive, so they did not have any there. But at the new Garden they had cakes and powdered beef and ale, 'and so home again by water with much pleasure'.

Occasional playgoing and excursions were not adequate expedients for ensuring that Elizabeth was contented. From the middle of 1662 onwards it must have become obvious to Pepys that he would have to take some comprehensive steps to deal with the problem of making Elizabeth's leisure hours tolerable and even pleasant. As he began to give his whole attention to his work, his time was increasingly occupied, so that Elizabeth saw no more of him then than she had done when he was largely intent on his own pleasures. At first he tried to persuade himself that she was contented, 'since she sees how I spend my time'. But the dilemma remained. For some months he shirked it, and failed to take adequate measures to grapple with his responsibilities. He actually felt aggrieved, and even angry, when he found that Elizabeth was scheming to have a female companion without consulting him; but he had to admit to himself that she 'do live very lonely'. He ruminated on the problem. 'But I must think of some way either to find her somebody to keep her company, or to set her to work, and by employment to take up her thoughts and time.' This certainly sounds both cold-blooded and half-hearted. Shortly afterwards, he was 'a little displeased with my wife, who, poor wretch, is troubled with her lonely life, which I know not how without great charge to help as yet, but I will study how to do it'. His frequently displayed unwillingness to spend money on such an object as making Elizabeth happy was a main cause of his failure to solve the ever-pressing difficulty. The idea occurred to him of taking his sister Pall (Paulina) into his household as Elizabeth's companion. The cost would be small. The experiment was tried, and was a failure, largely because Pall was not an easy person to fit into a family.

As time passed, and nothing effective was done, Elizabeth continued to make investigations on her own behalf. She was rash enough to try and coax Pepys by telling him of a possible companion 'that is pretty and can sing'. He was discreet, and appeared to be not 'over-forward' as a result of this information; 'but I see I must keep somebody for company's sake to my wife, for I am ashamed she should live as she do'. This was an improvement in his attitude; and soon an excellent person, Mary Ashwell, arrived. She could play on the harpsicon and the triangle (perhaps a kind of spinet), and proved, according to Pepys, to be 'a merry jade'. For nearly six months the problem was solved. Elizabeth had delightful company. They all three played cards together in the evenings; and Pepys arranged excursions and other pleasures, including the fateful dancing-lessons. Unfortunately, the girl had to leave because Elizabeth did not get on with her. But, in any case, Elizabeth's jealousy of Pepys's attentions to the girl would soon have produced the same result.

More than a year elapsed before a successor to Ashwell was employed. Meanwhile Elizabeth's dissatisfaction swelled up again with full force. While she had been away in the country Pepys arranged considerable alterations and improvements in the house; and the workmen naturally left the interior in a considerable state of dirtiness. Elizabeth told him that she believed that this was part of his plan for keeping her occupied at home. Secretly, he was bound to concede that there was a measure of truth in this accusation. Confinement 'within doors' was, as might be expected, a grievance that persisted in her mind for many months; and, once, when her feelings were exacerbated, she broke out in front of Pepys's friend, Creed. This predicament was one with which Pepys was unable to cope, for he could not, in that company, ride the high horse. The situation was, in fact, as he picturesquely put it, one 'which vexed me to the guts'.

It is hardly, perhaps, necessary to add that much of the discontinuity in the employment of female companions was due to Pepys's overfamiliarity with them. Mary Mercer, who arrived about a year after Ashwell's departure, was a most attractive girl. But before long it became obvious to Elizabeth that Pepys took an undue delight in her company, and also in her physical charms. He much enjoyed teaching her songs and music, but could not find the patience to do the same with his wife. There was the usual quarrel between mistress and companion, and a breach. It must have been galling to Elizabeth to find that when a charming female companion was in residence Pepys somehow found time to be at home much more than when the two of them were alone. He was fully conscious of the improved attractions of home-life when there was livelier entertainment available. Soon after he had noticed Mercer's charm and musical ability, as well as the musical ability of his new boy, he remarked that it was now becoming 'a constant pleasure to be at home'.

Elizabeth sometimes felt that she needed something more diverting than the conversation of an attendant; and it was for this reason that she persuaded Pepys to let her take dancing-lessons. She enjoyed them immensely; but they only lasted a few weeks; and thereafter she only had infrequent opportunities of using her skill. On thinking over what had best be done, Pepys decided that active employment in improving the interior of the house might keep her mind occupied, and at the same time prevent her from going out and about. She might, he thought, spend a considerable time improving the decorations of her study and their bedroom. He bought a chintz to line her study, and the next day, being a Sunday, 'she and I entertained one another all day long with great pleasure contriving about my wife's closet and the bedchamber'. On the Monday he was at the shops again, buying materials for decoration. For many days then Elizabeth was hard at work; and his plan was proving most effective. He did not merely admire, but spent some time helping. Her assiduity was admirable, as we learn from such entries in the Diary as this: '. . . my wife all day putting up her hangings in her closet which she do very prettily herself with her own hand, to my great content'.

But the decorations were soon completed; and he asked himself what he could do next to ensure her occupation or entertainment. He decided that he would enter on a course of teaching her arithmetic, and later the globes, including geography. This would seem to be a most unsuitable project. Elizabeth was of a spirited, sentimental, social turn of mind, and arithmetic was not an apt choice for satisfying her need for recreation. He started on the course with optimism; and she at least with goodwill. After the first lesson, he reported: 'She takes it very well, and, I hope, with great pleasure, I shall bring her to understand many fine things.' But it soon became obvious that these evening lessons could not remedy her loneliness during the daytime. She could not, or would not, practise arithmetic by herself. It did not keep her employed as did the interior house-decoration. But Pepys pressed on with the lessons; and Elizabeth managed to give an appearance of enjoying them. Perhaps she was happy because they were together; and he was trying to do something for her.

Pepys evidently felt that he was able to enjoy Elizabeth's company more keenly in the course of these lessons than he had been when there was no bond of interest between them. He described himself as taking great pleasure in her company, and living with her 'with great content'. After succeeding in teaching her addition, subtraction and multiplication, he decided that he would not proceed to division, but would transfer his tuition to astronomy and geography, and he accordingly discoursed to her 'upon the globes'. Sometimes the lessons took place after midday dinner. At one of these he read 'a lecture to her in Geography, which she takes very prettily, and with great pleasure to her and me to teach her'. Elizabeth's behaviour during these weeks is a notable tribute to her compliance and her affection for him. It is astonishing that she submitted to this schooling as long as she did.

A much better scheme, designed to occupy her leisure time in

Pepys's absence during the day, was that of learning to paint pictures. Lessons were arranged; and within two or three months she exceeded Pepys's most hopeful expectations. Her work was done 'very finely to my great satisfaction beyond what I could ever look for'. Somehow or another, this plan did not succeed. Her heart, it may be guessed, was not in it. There was not enough of human interest to satisfy her needs. Her practice of the art lasted through a summer and autumn; and, though she tried again for a short time in the next year, she did not settle to it.

The earlier project of interior house-decoration or upholstering of walls seemed to Pepys to be one which was worth attempting again. He 'pitched on' some blue damask 'very handsome', and Elizabeth started covering the walls of the bedchamber. For some weeks she worked 'like a horse' and 'like a drudge'; and Pepys was delighted. But, as before, the labour was soon completed; and some other occupation had to be sought, for he had not yet found any permanent solution to the great problem. And, early in 1667, she could still complain to him of being left alone and being kept 'within doors', which, he admitted, 'I do not well nor wisely in'.

It was in 1667, however, that Pepys made one of his best choices of diversion for Elizabeth. Although various experiments had shown that she had only very limited musical ability, he arranged for her to have lessons on the flageolet. A plan of this kind had several merits. She could practise during her leisure hours in the day-time; and they could play together in the evenings, thus providing a common interest that could unite them closely. Unfortunately, she had not a good ear, and, moreover, did not enjoy practising. Nevertheless, Pepys became 'pleased', 'mightily pleased', and 'infinitely pleased' with her efforts. And after a few weeks they played together, either after dinner or after supper; and in this capacity he described her as outdoing his expectations, an ambiguous expression. This happy collaboration lasted some four months. There is no doubt that Elizabeth tried hard. But it eventually became clear that his standards were too high for her.

In the same year she took lessons in singing. But here her lack of ear was a greater handicap; and at first his patience and restraint were sorely tried. When she sang a note out of tune, as she did now and then, he was irritated, and even experienced acute discomfort. He confessed that he had not patience enough to teach her, and recognized that he was intolerant, and failed to give her due encouragement. 'This I was troubled at, for I do find that I do put her out of heart, and make her fearfull to sing before me.' Again: 'Poor wretch! her ear is so bad that it made me angry, till the poor wretch cried to see me so vexed at her . . . She hath a great mind to learn, only to please me; and therefore, I am mighty unjust to her in discouraging her so much, but we were good friends . . .'

Elizabeth persisted in her endeavours, with great credit to herself; and Pepys thought that 'she will come to sing pretty well'. He began to gain 'some pleasure' from her singing. Later on, he could say that her ear had come to be more musical, 'which rejoices me to the heart, for I take great delight now to hear her sing'. After this, he spent several evenings with her singing and 'piping' on the flageolet, sometimes in the garden, it being summer. Mercer was often there, too. But she, being an excellent performer, made Elizabeth shy, especially as it became obvious that Elizabeth was less valued as a partner in music. In spite, however, of impediments, these occasions must have been among the happiest of their married life. It is a pity they did not extend over longer periods.

The preceding paragraphs might seem to imply that the social relations of the Pepyses were defective. This would be to some extent misleading. Many entries in the Diary indicate that they often enjoyed periods of intimate conversation. He went home to dinner with Elizabeth, for instance, 'very pleasant and pleased with one another's company'. The whole of a Sunday afternoon would be spent in casual chat. Another Sunday they were 'together all the evening discoursing'. Or they would spend time 'with great pleasure talking and discoursing of our late observations abroad'. Both in summer and winter they walked and talked together, either on the leads, or in the garden, generally in the evening, before or after supper; sometimes in the moonshine; and even under a frosty moon. Often they relished quiet conversation on going to bed, or in bed before getting up in the morning. There are several compendious entries such as: 'My wife and I lay very long in bed today talking and pleasing one another in discourse.' 'Lay with great content talking to my wife in bed.' The most accomplished diarist could not produce eloquent and colourful accounts of such habitual but infinitely valuable aspects of matrimony.

In spite of the accustomed converse between husband and wife which gave abundant pleasure to both parties, and in spite of the normal social activities in the home and elsewhere, Elizabeth was often lonely; and she was apt to complain that her life was lacking in diversion. Doubtless Pepys himself, by himself, could have solved Elizabeth's difficulties and made her contented if he had been more sensitive and perceptive. Above all, she wanted his affection, and must have known that, fundamentally, she had it. But she also wanted to have those frequent delicate attentions which are proof of a steady devotion. If only he had made it more obvious that he genuinely enjoyed her company, and, better still, if he could have convinced her that he preferred it to anyone else's, she might have been prepared to tolerate some hours of loneliness.

Towards the end of the Diary, Pepys's eyesight, which had been troubling him for some years, became so much impaired that he found the greatest difficulty in reading by candlelight. A few weeks before the attractive young companion of Elizabeth, Deb Willet, arrived, Elizabeth had been keeping him entertained in the evenings by reading books to him. She must have been patient and devoted, for the books were hardly such as to have much interest for her. Among others, there were 'Mr. Boyle's discourse on the style of the Scripture' and 'Sir R. Cotton's discourse of war'. After there had been sufficient time for the convulsions caused by Pepys's affair with Deb to subside, Elizabeth resumed her reading aloud. This practical fellowship must have served to mitigate the distresses recently suffered by both of them, and to show them the way to a gentler course of life together.

18

His Wife Under Close Control

In his schemes for occupying Elizabeth's leisure, and for keeping her satisfied with the manner of life that he thought it advisable or inevitable that she should lead, Pepys was acting partly as the thoughtful, kind-hearted mentor, partly as an interested party, and partly as a constitutional disciplinarian. He was to a large extent genuine, no doubt, in the solicitude he showed for Elizabeth's welfare. He was an interested party because he naturally liked her diversions to harmonize with his own. But his propensity to domineer was strongly marked. Her submissiveness was an essential part of their relationship, as he viewed it. He frequently remarked in the Diary that, if he gave her much freedom, she would become undisciplined and arrogant. Except when he lost his temper, he had no wish to humiliate her; but matrimony only ran smoothly if she was uniformly compliant.

She was, in fact, expected to be subject to his control to what seems today to be a preposterous extent. This is illustrated most markedly in his insistence on managing and regulating her dress and her expenditure of money. She was by no means free to clothe herself as she liked. She could not buy or even, on occasion, wear her clothes unless they met with his approval. We have already noticed that they had some serious quarrels on this subject, and that, on their way to church one Sunday, he disapproved of her dress, and she turned back home in natural protest against his arbitrary behaviour. He was accustomed to insist on having his way even in quite detailed matters. For instance, he told her that he was not willing for her 'to have her gowne laced, but would lay out the same money and more on a plain new one'. The continuation of this story illustrates the pitch to which their wrangling could reach. 'At this [his dictatorial resolve] she flounced away in a manner I never saw her, nor which I could ever endure. So I away to the office, though she had dressed herself to go see my Lady Sandwich. She by and by in a rage follows me, and coming to me tells me in a spitefull manner like a vixen and with a look full of rancour that she would go buy a new one and lace it and make me pay for it, and then let me burn it if I would after she had done it, and so went away in a fury. This vexed me cruelly, but being very busy I had not hand to give myself up to consult what to do in it, but anon, I suppose after she saw that I did not follow her, she came again to the office, where I made her stay, being busy with another, half an houre, and her stomach coming down we were presently friends, and so after my business being over at the office we out and by coach to my Lady Sandwich's . . .' His description of the scene is extraordinarily vivid and revealing.

Any mode of dress which seemed to him to tend to immodesty in his wife aroused his ire. What may have been a somewhat daring costume provoked an outburst. 'I being displeased with her cutting away a lace handkercher sewed about her neck down to her breasts almost, out of a belief, but without reason, that it is the fashion. Here we did give one another the lie too much, but were presently friends.'

There was another unhappy day when he refused to accompany her attired in a dress of which he disapproved. 'Anon comes down my wife, dressed in her second mourning, with her black moyre waistcoat, and short petticoat, laced with silver lace so basely that I could not endure to see her, and with laced lining which is too soon, so that I was horrid angry, and went out of doors to the office and there staid, and would not go to our intended meeting, which vexed me to the blood, and my wife sent twice or thrice to me, to direct her any way to dress her, but to put on her cloth

gown, which she would not venture; which made me mad . . .'
The next day he saw things in a fairer light, and wrote: 'I . . .
think I did give her as much cause to be angry with me.'

Pepys's control extended not only to the kind of clothes Elizabeth
wore, but to the buying of them, and the price paid for them. He
used to accompany her on some of her shopping expeditions so as
to approve of what she bought. He went 'with her from shop to
shop laying out near £10 this morning on clothes for her'.
If he did not accompany her, he had to approve the purchases
afterwards. For instance, after he had 'looked over the things my
wife had bought today, which being not very well pleased with,
they costing too much, I went to bed in a discontent'. When,
however, Elizabeth rebelled against his treatment of her as a child,
his manner was softened. He walked in the garden with her in the
evening, 'and there scolded a little, I being doubtful that she had
received a couple of fine pinners (one of point de Gesne), which I
feared she hath from some [one] or other of a present; but on the
contrary, I find she hath bought them for me to pay for them,
without my knowledge. This do displease me much; but yet do so
much please me better than if she had received them the other way,
that I was not much angry, and fell to other discourse . . .'

Until almost the end of the period of the Diary he would not
trust Elizabeth with an allowance, but handed out money piecemeal,
as he approved of its expenditure. Even as late as 1666 she had to
ask him for money to spend, as she was going out shopping with
Lady Penn; and, three days later: 'My wife snappish because I
denied her money to lay out this afternoon; however, good friends
again . . .' Elizabeth, after much pressure, finally succeeded in
persuading him to make her an allowance. He was backward in
giving way, never liking to part with money; but in the end he
undertook of his own accord to give her £30 a year, which pleased
her, 'it being more than ever she asked for or expected'.

Not merely dress, in the sense of clothes, but all matters relating
to her personal appearance came under his review and control. She
could not wear a black patch on her face without his leave. 'My
wife seemed very pretty today, it being the first time I had given

her leave to wear a black patch.' Anything artificial in the way of adornment of the face angered him, as we have noticed. Elizabeth, complying with the prevailing fashion, began to wear a pair of peruques of hair 'which are pretty, and are of my wife's hair, or else I should not endure them'. Much later, she evidently wore these artificial locks, but of white colour, not being made of her own hair. He became very angry and said he would not permit her to wear them. The quarrel ended in a compromise. He bought her some expensive lace in return for her promise not to wear white locks as long as he lived.

Elizabeth was, as we might suppose, expected to keep accurate accounts. He examined these from time to time, and pointed out errors. She was, it seems, not good at figures, and admitted to him one day that if she inadvertently forgot to enter an item of expenditure, she added something to other items to make it up. This made him cross. But she thought that he was finicky, and grew indignant, telling him that she would manage to lay by some money to buy a necklace, 'which madded me and do still trouble me'.

Money was at the root of most of his ungenerous behaviour about his wife's dress and other expenses. In the first year or two of his appointment as a Navy Commissioner, although he spent freely on his own amusements, he certainly had not much money to spare. But after four years he could, we may suppose, have been more open-handed with Elizabeth than he was. It was not until about seven or eight years had passed that he began to be liberal.

A succession of incidents spread over the years of the Diary can be made to provide a revealing commentary on his close-fisted proceedings. In 1661, on going to church with Elizabeth, her mourning dress looked so old that he was ashamed to be seen with her. The fault was his. It is clear that he was neglecting to give her proper clothes, for in the next month Lady Sandwich took him to task. She had evidently noticed Elizabeth's shabby appearance, and she 'did mightily urge' him to spend some money on her dress, 'so I seemed to be pleased with it, and do resolve to bestow a lace upon her'. Lady Sandwich reiterated her advice on the following day, 'which I think it best for me to do for her honour and my own'. The day after that he found that Lady Sandwich had chosen a lace costing £6 for him to give Elizabeth, 'which I seemed much glad of that it was no more, though in my mind I think it too much, and I pray God to keep me to order myself and my wife's expenses that no inconvenience in purse or honour follow this my prodigality'. There is a good deal of information available to readers of the Diary to enable them to consider whether Pepys's attitude was a reasonable one.

A year later he 'sat talking with my wife about our entertaining Dr. Clerke's lady and Mrs. Pierce shortly, being in great pain that my wife hath never a winter gown, being almost ashamed of it, that she should be seen in a taffeta one, when all the world wears moyre [mohair]; so to prayers and to bed, but we could not come to any resolution what to do therein, other than to appear as she is'. But circumstances forced him to give way, and to be less parsimonious. He had, a few days afterwards, been extremely unkind to Elizabeth in destroying many of her private papers; and some reconciliation was imperative. The day for the entertainment had been fixed; and 'at last for my honour am forced to make her presently a new Moyre gown to be seen by Mrs. Clerke, which troubles me to part with so much money, but, however, it sets my wife and I to friends again . . .'

Some months after this he told a somewhat similar story; but the sequel was a little delayed. 'This morning I put on my best black cloth suit, trimmed with scarlett ribbon, very neat, with my cloake lined with velvett, and a new beaver, which altogether is very noble, with my black silk knit canons I bought a month ago. I to church alone, my wife not going, and there I found my Lady Batten in a velvet gown, which vexed me that she should be in it before my wife, or that I am able to put her into one, but what cannot be, cannot be. However, when I came home I told my wife of it, and to see my weaknesse, I could on the sudden have found [it in] my heart to have offered her one, but second thoughts put it by, and indeed it would undo me to think of doing as Sir W. Batten and his Lady do, who has a good estate besides his office.' Elizabeth had to wait four months for a rich dress. At last, her gown, laced, was delivered, 'which is indeed very handsome, but it will cost me a great deal of money, more than ever I intended, but it is for once'. This expenditure fretted him; and the subject was discussed by Elizabeth and himself the next evening. 'Lay long in bed wrangling with my wife about the charge she puts me to at this time for clothes, more than I intended, and very angry we were, but quickly friends again.'

There had been a few months earlier another example of the way in which Lady Sandwich had to force him to be heedful of Elizabeth's appearance. It was by her advice that application was made from the country for a 'very pretty' silk petticoat. Pepys hastened to send 'a very fine rich one . . . much better than she desires or expects'. He was a little afraid of Lady Sandwich.

More or less constant pressure for more liberal treatment was maintained by Elizabeth. He managed to put off an unwelcome application by promising to give her £20 at a date well into the future. The day arrived, 'but [I] did boggle mightily at the parting with my money, but at last did give it to her . . .'

Even as late as 1667 he was still holding the purse-strings tightly. At a time when he was worth about £7,000, he remarked that his wife was 'mighty pressing for a new pair of cuffs, which I am against the laying out of money upon yet, which makes her angry'. But, as often, Elizabeth managed to secure her ends by exercising patience and insistence at the same time. And, two days later, he described her as looking 'very fine today, in her suit of laced cuffs and perquisites'.

Near the end of the Diary period he could treat her generously; but he could also still be calculating. Everyone agrees that he never ceased to be in love with her; but he hardly ever seems to have been so carried away by his love that he was prepared to give her, rashness apart, whatever she wanted. This parsimony persisted. In 1667 he had his wife as one of his Valentines; and he remarked that this would cost him £5; but he added that he must have spent that sum on her anyhow, even if she had not been his Valentine, so that he would not be at a loss by it.

The next year they again played at being young lovers, and she was to be his Valentine. His gift was to be a ring of Turkey stone set with little sparks of diamonds. He observed that he was 'not much troubled at it. It will cost me near £5—she costing me but little compared with other wives, and I have not many occasions to spend on her.' But, in fact, he, at this time, spent 'above £4' on a dressing-box and other things for her chamber and table.

It was about then that, one evening, 'my wife did with great pleasure shew me her stock of jewells, encreased by the ring . . . and, with this and what she had, she reckons that she hath about £150 worth of jewells, of one kind or another; and I am glad of it, for it is fit the wretch should have something to content herself with'. It should be remembered to his credit that he freely gave her a pearl necklace costing £80 in 1666; and it is this that helped most to bring the total to £150.

Many incidents quoted above may easily lead to the impression that Elizabeth had scarcely any reputable dresses, and that Pepys was not desirous of seeing her richly and attractively dressed. In fact, there are numerous references which suggest that from time to time she was in possession of a reasonable wardrobe. He often describes her as 'very pretty' in a new dress, such as her 'slasht wastecoat', a 'green petticoat of flowred satin, with fine white and gimp lace of her own putting on', a 'new laced gowne' that 'becomes her very nobly', and 'a new suit of flowered ash-coloured silke, very noble'. In church, she was 'very fine in a new yellow bird's-eye hood, as the fashion is now'. As time went on the dresses became more handsome and expensive, as a result of Pepys's enlarged finances. She wore 'her velvett vest, which is mighty fine, and becomes her exceedingly'. And when she was anxious to drive out with her husband in their new and splendid coach, she wore her 'flowered tabby gown'. He thought her looking 'extraordinary fine'; and 'everybody in love with it'.

19

Compunction

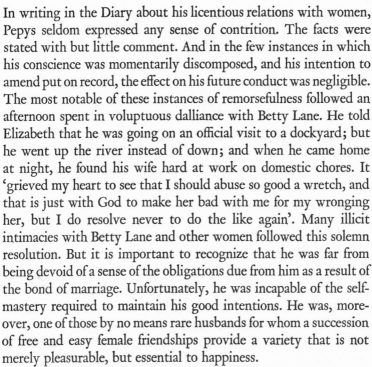

In writing in the Diary about his licentious relations with women, Pepys seldom expressed any sense of contrition. The facts were stated with but little comment. And in the few instances in which his conscience was momentarily discomposed, and his intention to amend put on record, the effect on his future conduct was negligible. The most notable of these instances of remorsefulness followed an afternoon spent in voluptuous dalliance with Betty Lane. He told Elizabeth that he was going on an official visit to a dockyard; but he went up the river instead of down; and when he came home at night, he found his wife hard at work on domestic chores. It 'grieved my heart to see that I should abuse so good a wretch, and that is just with God to make her bad with me for my wronging her, but I do resolve never to do the like again'. Many illicit intimacies with Betty Lane and other women followed this solemn resolution. But it is important to recognize that he was far from being devoid of a sense of the obligations due from him as a result of the bond of marriage. Unfortunately, he was incapable of the self-mastery required to maintain his good intentions. He was, moreover, one of those by no means rare husbands for whom a succession of free and easy female friendships provide a variety that is not merely pleasurable, but essential to happiness.

As Elizabeth never knew anything about the many sordid intrigues that Pepys indulged in, there was no question of her expecting him to acknowledge his error and ask her forgiveness. There was no quarrel to compose, and no need for him to express his compunction to her. But, where the inconsiderateness or unkindness in his behaviour to Elizabeth was obvious, it was another matter. She must have found it particularly exasperating that he was so little inclined to assume any responsibility for their dissensions; and the main responsibility was usually his. In writing in his Diary about disagreements with his wife, Pepys frequently admitted that he had acted unjustifiably; but, as far as we know, he only admitted it to himself. He never says that he apologized, except in the sad affair of Deb.

Soon after the Deb episode Elizabeth threatened to leave him. This had the effect of frightening him thoroughly, and of extracting from him added expressions of guilt and penitence. He did not want to lose her: indeed, he would have been lost without her. But there was another motive for his submissiveness. He had a keen desire for the esteem of his friends and acquaintances. How silly, and worse, how undignified he would look if it became known that his wife had found good reason to discard him! He doubtless applied principles that were consistent with his views on behaviour: marital dissensions that could be kept private were likely to assume no great importance; but a risk of their becoming public must be avoided at almost any cost, even that of self-abasement.

We have already noticed some occasions when, in recording quarrels with Elizabeth in which he had behaved badly, he avowed regret, in the privacy of the Diary. There are some other instances which should be mentioned in fairness to so frank an autobiographer. Angry disputes about Elizabeth's manner of dress and her expenditure on clothes and other articles were described in the Diary so as to make it clear that he recognized that his behaviour had been unduly harsh. For instance, he scolded her for not being 'fine enough' to go to a christening; but it proved that she was ill and miserable, and had a good excuse. He confessed to himself that he was in an ill humour, and that he felt ashamed.

His jealousy of Elizabeth's supposed intimacies with other men was unfounded and ridiculous; and he really knew that this was so.

Reviewing one of the most absurd of his suspicions, that of Pembleton, the dancing-master, he saw that it was a situation 'for which I
am truly to be blamed', and that Elizabeth and he had not, as a
result of it, 'the kindness between us which we used and ought to
have . . .' But his misgivings persisted; and he continued to have
cause to regret his self-delusion.

It might be thought that an habitually jealous husband would
be the last to give his wife cause to be jealous of him. On many
occasions Pepys provided Elizabeth with good grounds for being
aggrieved as a result of his marked preference for the company of
some of his female friends. He often admitted to himself that he was
acting improperly in this respect; and he decided that he would
remedy his errant ways. But these admissions and decisions do not
seem to have produced any noticeably beneficial results. One of
Elizabeth's companions, for instance, Mary Ashwell, a lively,
intelligent, accomplished girl, was paid marked attention by
Pepys; and naturally Elizabeth became indignant, because she
seemed to be neglected in favour of her attendant. Pepys owned to
himself that this interpretation of the facts was inescapable, 'and
I to blame; but for the time to come I will take care to remedy all'.
But, after a few days, he conceded that he was 'taken up in my talk
with Ashwell, who is a very witty girl'. He also acknowledged, in
the Diary, that he was not so fond of Elizabeth as he used to be, and
ought to be, which he must remedy. But he evidently did not cease
to show partiality for Ashwell; and, after an employment of a few
months, Elizabeth insisted on her dismissal.

Besides being caused unhappiness by Pepys's excessive interest
in the companions, Elizabeth was excusably jealous of two of his
women friends, Mrs. Pierce and Mrs. Knepp, of whom we have
spoken. The former had a considerable reputation for beauty, and
the latter possessed a high degree of charm together with the social
accomplishments characteristic of her profession as an actress. She
had the ability to sing supremely well, which put poor Elizabeth at
a disadvantage. These two, with more mature qualities than those
of the companions, gave Pepys considerable pleasure by their wit
and vivacity. They had, it was evident, much sprightlier minds

than Elizabeth. Pepys was most indiscreet in showing preference
for their conversation when all four were together. Elizabeth sometimes sulked; and sometimes had what revenge she could afterwards by telling Pepys they were whores and the like. One of the
most outrageous of his indiscretions was to reprove Elizabeth in
front of the other two for telling dull stories and making silly
remarks. Nothing could have been more injudicious, discourteous,
and even insulting. 'I find my wife troubled still at my checking her
last night in the coach in her long stories out of Grand Cyrus, which
she would tell, though nothing to the purpose, nor in a good
manner. This she took unkindly, and I think I was to blame indeed;
but she do find with reason, that in the company of Pierce, Knipp
and other women that I love, I do not value her, or mind her as I
ought.' A second entry in the Diary, made a few weeks later, shows
that his recognition of his blameworthiness had but little effect
when similar situations recurred. 'My wife,' he wrote, 'in a chagrin
humour, she not being pleased with my kindnesse to either of
them [Mrs. Pierce and Mrs. Knepp], and by and by she fell into
some silly discourse wherein I checked her which made her mighty
pettish.'

In the privacy of the Diary, Pepys could make wide admissions
of his culpability; and very often matters rested there without the
proper sequel. Perhaps the wider the admissions the less likely they
were to have effect on his behaviour. After harassing Elizabeth
about a small mistake which she had made in her household
accounts, he wrote: 'I indeed too angrily insisting on so poor a
thing . . . and the truth is I do find that my being over-solicitous
and jealous and froward and ready to reproach her do make her
worse.' His self-analysis was theoretical rather than practical.
Nevertheless, he eventually made some commendable efforts to
act on the principles that he enunciated in the Diary. These did not
quickly convert him into anything like a perfect husband. But a
tendency to improvement is noticeable over the years. In many
respects he is seen to be more considerate in the concluding period
of his marriage. If the episode of Deb had occurred five years
earlier, he might not have proved as submissive as he did.

20

Seeing Himself

Sometimes, it seems, Pepys was overactive in suspecting his inadequacies, both in regard to his wife and to others. Once when he and Elizabeth were in bed at night she was awake for some hours with severe pain from the gripes. 'I did find that I was most desirous to take my rest than to ease her, but there was nothing I could do her any good with.' In these circumstances his wife would hardly have wished him to keep awake; and his retrospective concern that he might not have maintained a proper standard of behaviour was superfluous. His anxious temperament, in fact, made him unduly troubled in case he had not been sufficiently sympathetic. Again, he heard that his father-in-law was seriously ill; but he was not satisfied with making a simple and sincere statement that he was sorry. He had to admit to himself that he was not as much concerned as he felt he should be. It was much the same with the death of his brother, Tom. He was distressed to see him dying and dead; but, as soon as the funeral was over, he allowed that he had 'very little grief indeed for him'. Some of his remarks about Tom suggest that he had but slight reason for grief, and that he was reproaching himself unnecessarily.

He also vexed himself in regard to his behaviour to people to whom he did not owe the same kind of obligation that he did to his relations. In considering his attitude to Mrs. Batters, the widow of a Captain Batters who had been drowned on naval duty, he wrote:

'I pity her, and will do her what kindness I can; yet I observe something of ill-nature in myself more than should be, that I am colder towards her in my charity than I should be to one so painful [attentive] as he and she have been and full of kindness to their power to my wife and I.'

He was active in searching his conscience, being scrupulous in discerning perversities and inconsistencies in his conduct. He sometimes suspected that he should have lent money when he had refused to do so; and, in particular, he noticed that he was most unwilling to part with money when he was most concerned in making it.

Not only in his attempts at self-analysis, but in his straight-forward factual accounts of his behaviour, Pepys has undoubtedly left us a distorted picture of his character by laying too much emphasis on his defects, and by failing, unavoidably no doubt, to disclose sufficiently his more endearing qualities. We can only infer such qualities from the Diary to a limited extent.

Why, we may ask, should Pepys have constantly recorded incidents which put him in a bad light? This is one of the major puzzles with which he has presented us. Perhaps he was so much engrossed in the delight of portraying the details of his story that he did not realize that he might appear as a very dubious celebrity. Artists with a fondness for accurate representation often fail to stand back from their work and comprehend the general effect. But if he perused several paragraphs he could hardly gain pleasure from regarding so inglorious a portrait.

It is conceivable but unlikely that he was meticulous in describing the deficiencies in his character in order that he might contemplate them, and thus plan to improve his standards of behaviour. Or he may have written in this way in order that he might, so to speak, get the trouble out of his system, a sort of moral purgation or catharsis. The unblushing way in which he gives particulars of some of his imperfections discourages these hypotheses.

He may have had several objects in writing the Diary and seeing to its preservation. We know that he regarded it as being capable of providing effective evidence to vindicate him in case he was charged with irregularities in his office. But if it got into other people's hands it might have had an opposite effect, for it included numerous facts damaging to his professional reputation. Another imaginable object is the retrospective enjoyment of pleasant and gratifying experiences, though indications that he re-read the Diary from time to time are small. Alternatively, we may ascribe his motive to the actual enjoyment of literary composition of this kind, being for him perhaps a particularly satisfying means of self-expression.

A possible explanation seems to be that, as an exceptionally broadminded man, he hoped that when he was dead his Diary might, after a proper interval, be made public; and as a result its readers could have a more intimate view of an interesting fellow human than had ever been available before. It can, then, be argued that he was unsparing in his self-disclosures because he wanted his representation of himself to be one that was unprecedentedly authentic and convincing. He might be prepared to risk exciting some disapprobation in regard to certain aspects of his behaviour as long as he felt that his unrestraint would enable the portrait to have singularity and, perhaps, a kind of pre-eminence. Though he can hardly have contemplated the chance of achieving immortality, he might have nurtured a hope that discriminating persons would find in his Diary some unique and fascinating features.

There are those who, after a due consideration of the contents of the Diary, say that Pepys could not possibly have intended it to be published. These suppositions may be expressed too categorically and may fail to recognize the width of his outlook. There are also those who contend that, as he did not leave instructions for publication, he must have desired secrecy. But how do we know that he did not leave such instructions? He did not use his last will and testament for this purpose, because he would naturally have wished the instructions to be confidential. If he gave separate, private instructions, they may have been neglected or overlooked. However this may be, it is important to bear in mind that when he bequeathed his library, including the Diary, well bound and catalogued, he took no steps, as far as we know, to ensure non-publication; and the key to the shorthand (not cipher, as has been sometimes supposed) had been published in a book, a copy of which was in his bequeathed library.[1]

A good many scraps of internal evidence suggest that the Diary was written so as to be suitable for others to read in due course, when transcribed. These are chiefly phrases stating facts so well known to the diarist that he would hardly have included them for his own benefit.[2] And there is very little in the Diary that is not perfectly understandable by any reader, apart from the mention of a very few people whose identity is not made clear. A diary written entirely for himself would probably have had numerous perplexing allusions.

Pepys was not, perhaps, as interested as we are in the diverse aspects of his character. It was that of a strenuous and conscientious official who was apt to succumb to the seduction of making dubious profits, and now and then to be unduly enticed by the allurements of pleasure; excitable and impetuous in personal relations, yet steady and industrious in business; a strong strain of Puritanism in him combined with an astonishing, even prodigious passion for the courting of women; kindly, but calculating; possessed of a tender sympathy, the value of which must have been diminished, in his relations with his wife, by occasional inconsiderateness; at the same time both lavish and sparing in his expenditure; utterly resolute in the last resort, but sometimes unduly anxious, and capable of timidity in the face of physical danger.

He probably had an indistinct appreciation of these conflicting

[1] Thomas Shelton, *Tachygraphy*.

[2] E.g. III 9. 'Hither comes Major Tolhurst, one of my old acquaintances in Cromwells' time, and sometimes of our Clubb, to see me . . .'

III 47. 'within the Merchant's Gate, under which we pass to go into our garden . . .'

III 197. 'thence to my Viall maker's in Bishopsgate Street; his name is Wise . . .'

IV 394–5. 'Jack Cole, my old schoole-fellow, is dead . . . who was a great crony of mine.' (The references are to the *Diary*, ed. H. B. Wheatley, in eight volumes.)

There are some dozens of other similar instances to be found in the Diary.

It is especially remarkable that Pepys always referred to Elizabeth as 'my wife'. Surely any diarist writing for himself alone would refer to his wife by her Christian name, or some modification of it.

features. But he was well aware of the desirability of keeping his behaviour under review. He liked to be liked; and he was constantly prepared to recognize his defects, being anxious to deserve a good reputation. Nevertheless, we may sometimes conclude that, while admirable at self-examination, he was not so successful at the complementary aspect of this practice. In this, however, he was by no means peculiar. He has many claims to be thought an estimable person. If devotion to his country's service and enlargement of the happiness of many human beings are critical tests, he certainly satisfied them.

Some of the problems raised by the Diary can provide opportunities for pleasurable investigation. Not only can we try to understand why Pepys wrote and preserved so intimate a record of his doings and impressions, with disclosures that sometimes make him unlikeable or ridiculous, we can also dwell on the puzzling aspects of his character, and try to answer some of the questions raised by a study of it. Was he honest with himself? Was he unduly pleased with himself? It is easy to find examples of his conviction that he was an administrator of outstanding ability. When he asserted that the main reasons for his success were diligence, punctuality, and an attention to detail, was he aping a modesty that he never possessed? He sometimes defended himself against possible charges of dishonesty. Was he convinced of what he alleged, or was he indulging in essays in exculpation? How far did he consider that his arbitrary treatment of his wife was justified, or salutary?

Most of these questions are of a kind that Pepys himself could not possibly have answered. As regards the rest, so intuitive were many of his actions, and so sophistical some of his reasoning, that he might not have been able to enlighten an inquirer, even if he had been willing to do so. No one can see his own merits and demerits in proper perspective. But Pepys opened his mind so liberally and exhaustively in the Diary, that, in certain respects, it may be possible for its readers to know more about him than he did about himself.

Index